William Justin Harsha

Sabbath-Day Journeys

A study of the thirty-third chapter of Numbers

William Justin Harsha
Sabbath-Day Journeys
A study of the thirty-third chapter of Numbers
ISBN/EAN: 9783744755306

Printed in Europe, USA, Canada, Australia, Japan

Cover: Foto ©Suzi / pixelio.de

More available books at **www.hansebooks.com**

SABBATH-DAY JOURNEYS

A STUDY OF THE THIRTY-THIRD CHAPTER OF NUMBERS

BY THE

Rev. WILLIAM JUSTIN HARSHA, D.D.

PASTOR OF THE SECOND COLLEGIATE REFORMED CHURCH
OF HARLEM, NEW YORK CITY

FLEMING H. REVELL COMPANY

NEW YORK   CHICAGO   TORONTO

Publishers of Evangelical Literature

FOREWORD

The thirty-third chapter of Numbers has commonly been regarded as a desert place in the Word. Few Bible students care to tarry long in its apparently dry and unfruitful wastes. The following series of studies is an attempt to show how unfounded this wide-spread opinion is. Every part of God's Word is "profitable," and the chapter referred to is not among the least useful and instructive portions. The significance of Bible names is nowhere shown more clearly. The work of sanctification in the soul is not elsewhere more strikingly portrayed.

It is to be noted that special value is attached to this chapter by the statement of its second verse: "Moses wrote their goings out according to their journeys by the commandment of the Lord." This catalogue of the stations of Israel in the desert was made in obedience to a direct command of God. It will be observed that just forty-two journeys are mentioned here. This is significant, since forty-two is the number used in Scripture of the period of trial and discipline through which the church or an individual is called upon to pass. Then when we discover that the name of each station is significant, and that, taken in order, the journeys beautifully set forth the whole course of the Christian from sin's bondage to the heavenly Canaan, we are led to understand why this chapter is given so prominent a place in the Word.

The example of our Lord and of His apostles may be pleaded as authority for the method of interpretation employed. Particularly may an appeal be made to 1 Corinthians, the tenth chapter, and most particularly to the sixth verse of the chapter: "Now these things were our examples;" or, as it is rendered in the margin of the Revised Version, "In these things they became figures of us." What befell the Israelites in the desert is a sublime and beautiful panorama of the work of grace in the human heart. All the trials and sufferings, as well as the joys and encouragements, of the Christian's training are here prefigured. It is not to be wondered at that Marah and Elim, Rephidim and Sinai, and many other stations appear repeatedly in the church's hymns and homilies. A closer study should yield added, if not more precious, results.

Thankful acknowledgment is made to Mr. Thomas Bromley, of England, whose little treatise on the desert stations, published nearly a century and a half ago and long since out of print, has been of material aid to the author. Many of his interpretations of names have been adopted, and it is hoped that his devout spirit has been followed. Other names and authorities need scarcely be mentioned. The aim of the book is distinctly practical, and it is hardly possible that any one who takes it into his hands will care to dispute upon fine points of etymology. Out of the storehouse have been drawn "things new and old." Into this small garner Christian students are invited to enter and take as their need shall be, giving the blessed Master all honor.

Of the forty-two journeys there have been made fifty-two studies. The hope is that a quiet hour on the Sabbath day will be devoted to a careful reading of each section in turn, with a prayerful meditation upon the illustrative passages suggested. This hope prompted the giving of the name to the book. The studies will carry one through a year if pursued in this manner. Yet there is nothing arbitrary in the arrangement. This is not a Sabbath text-book for any given year. The study may be begun at any time and may be prosecuted at any desired rate of speed. The author has had in mind those busy workers who might be able to devote an hour on the Lord's day to following the pilgrims in a pilgrim spirit. He prays that this little book may be a blessing to such, to all, indeed, who take it into their hands, and, warm with this prayer, he sends it forth to its mission under the guidance of the Holy Spirit.

CONTENTS

		PAGE
	Foreword	7
I.	Rameses	15
II.	Succoth	21
III.	Etham	26
IV.	Pi-hahiroth	32
V.	Marah	37
VI.	Elim	42
VII.	Red Sea	46
VIII.	Wilderness of Sin	51
IX.	Dophkah	55
X.	Alush	61
XI.	Rephidim	66
XII.	Sinai	71
XIII.	Kibroth-hattaavah	77
XIV.	Hazeroth	81
XV.	Rithmah	85
XVI.	Rimmon-parez	90

		PAGE
XVII.	LIBNAH	95
XVIII.	RISSAH	99
XIX.	KEHELATHAH	104
XX.	SHAPHER	109
XXI.	HARADAH	114
XXII.	MAKHELOTH	119
XXIII.	TAHATH	125
XXIV.	TARAH	131
XXV.	MITHCAH	137
XXVI.	HASHMONAH	142
XXVII.	MOSEROTH	146
XXVIII.	BENE-JAAKAN	151
XXIX.	HOR-HAGIDGAD	155
XXX.	JOTBATHAH	160
XXXI.	EBRONAH	165
XXXII.	EZION-GABER	170
XXXIII.	KADESH	175
XXXIV.	KADESH (*Continued*)	180
XXXV.	MOUNT HOR	185
XXXVI.	ZALMONAH	189
XXXVII.	PUNON	193
XXXVIII.	OBOTH	199
XXXIX.	IJE-ABARIM	204
XL.	DIBON-GAD	210
XLI.	ALMON-DIBLATHAIM	215
XLII.	MOUNTAINS OF ABARIM	219
XLIII.	PLAINS OF MOAB	224

		PAGE
XLIV.	Plains of Moab—Pitching before Jordan	230
XLV.	Plains of Moab—In Contact with the Moabites	236
XLVI.	Plains of Moab—In Conflict with the Midianites	241
XLVII.	Plains of Moab—The Repetition of the Law	247
XLVIII.	Plains of Moab—The Investiture of Joshua	253
XLIX.	Plains of Moab—The Prayer of Moses	257
L.	Plains of Moab—The Vision of Moses	262
LI.	Plains of Moab—The Death of Moses	267
LII.	Plains of Moab—The Mourning for Moses	271

SABBATH-DAY JOURNEYS

I

RAMESES

WHEN God had made all arrangements to lead His chosen people out from Egypt, the command was given to the Israelites to assemble in Rameses (Num. xxxiii. 1–4). This was one of the districts of Egypt convenient for starting upon the journey to the Promised Land. We read of it first in Genesis xlvii. 11, where it is stated that Joseph caused his father and brethren to settle there, "in the best of the land," when they first came to Egypt. It was a fertile district, lying at the foot of the beautiful hills almost opposite the pyramids on the other side of the Nile. Up in the mountains behind the foot-hills was the village of On, whose priest, or prince, was Poti-pherah (Gen. xli. 45). It was the daughter of this priest who was given to Joseph to wife. Other villages of this district were Aven, or Heliopolis (Ezek. xxx. 17), and Beth-shemesh, of which we read frequently in the Scriptures. Hence this district was interesting in itself, as well as made memorable by the rendezvous of the Israelites as they started for

Canaan. As it was the first place on which their feet rested in Egypt, so it was to be the place whence the return to the Land of Promise should begin—a very significant fact. God often brings us back to the first things and the first places in our spiritual life in order to admonish and advance us on our way. When Joseph and Mary lost the child Jesus they went straight back to the place where they had had Him last. So when we have lost our peace or our testimony must we go back to the point—the temptation or the failure—where we let it slip. There by true penitence may we take it to us again.

Every family that would be saved from destruction in Egypt was required to hasten to this place of rendezvous. No one would be allowed to reach Canaan without passing through Rameses. This command was imperative and without exception. Now the literal meaning of the word " Rameses " is the " melting " or " washing away of evil." As the cold snows of the late springtime are melted away by the bright beams of the returning sun, so was sin in its deadly chill to be melted or washed away from the starting pilgrims. How beautifully does this reveal that the very first place whereon the soul must stand, when it would escape the Egypt of bondage and corruption, is upon the spot where the blood of Christ is applied in the washing away of sin! The journey to the heavenly Canaan must begin at the foot of the cross.

It may be instructive to turn to the following passages in order to substantiate this interpretation of the word " Rameses," which is compounded of *ra* (" evil ") and *meses* (*masah*) (" to melt "). *Ra* is used in Genesis ii. 9, Exodus v. 19, Leviticus xxvi. 6, Numbers xx. 5, Deuteronomy i. 35, Joshua xxiii. 15, Judges ii. 11, 2 Samuel iii. 39, and in something like five hundred other passages. *Masah* is used in Exodus xvi. 21, Joshua ii. 11, 2 Samuel xvii. 10, Psalms lxviii. 2, xcvii. 5, Isaiah xix. 1, and many other passages. There is also a very beautiful use of the word in Judges xv. 14, marg. This is a good illustration of the mystical truth in the word " Rameses "; for as the bonds " melted from off " the hands of Samson, so do the bonds of iniquity dissolve from our souls when the blood of Christ is applied.

Clearly it will be seen that, with careful thought for times then present and for all the future, God prepared for the journey of the Israelites to the Promised Land. Had it been a matter merely of taking six hundred thousand men, besides women and children, to Canaan, Omnipotence could easily have accomplished it. But the moral influence of the journey upon succeeding ages needed to be considered. It was a complicated problem, and resulted in a complicated journey. God Himself explains what He had in His heart when He says, " 'Thou shalt remember all the way which the Lord thy God led thee these forty years in the wilderness, to humble thee, and to prove thee, to know what was in thine heart, whether thou wouldest keep His commandments, or no " (Deut. viii. 2).

The people were at Rameses when the Passover was instituted and the last stroke of punishment fell upon the Egyptians. (See Exod. xii.) Immediately after this night of destruction Israel marched out, as is stated in the third verse of Numbers xxxiii.: " On the morrow after the Passover the children of Israel went out with a high hand in the sight of all the Egyptians." The Passover being really a type of our escape from the effects of sin by cleansing in the blood, we see how appropriate it was that it should be instituted at this first station, which means a " washing away of evil."

What then may we know as to the washing away of our sins in the blood of Christ?

1. He was manifested for that purpose (1 John iii. 5).

2. He Himself provides the redemption blood (1 Pet. i. 18, 19; Lev. xvi. 14, 15).

3. His blood is applied once for all (Heb. ix. 7–26). Notice the twelve references to blood application in these few verses.

4. His blood is perpetual and preserving (Exod. xii. 7, 13; Mark xiv. 23, 24). Notice Christ's own valuation of His blood (Matt. xxvi. 28).

5. This washing is a definite process which each one can recognize (1 Cor. vi. 11).

6. While there is but the one application of the blood for justification, there is a continued application for sanctification unto holiness (Rev. vii. 14). There is a beautiful passage in Ephesians v. 26, referring to the cleansing of justification, where the translation should be, as in the Revised Version, " That He might sanctify it, having cleansed it." The washing of justification precedes the process of sanctification.

7. The crowning glory of the risen Lord, as seen by John on Patmos, is still that He " loveth us," in that He hath " washed us *in* His own blood " (Rev. i. 5, R. V., marg.). The washing of justification is past, but

the love continues, and is shown more and more in sanctification.

Let us notice that we need often to be cleansed of things which we pride ourselves upon. This thought is brought out in Psalm xxxix. 11: "When Thou with rebukes dost correct man for iniquity, Thou makest that which is to be desired in him to melt away" (marg.). The word here is the root from which *meses* comes. This is precisely the thought of this first station of our journey, however humbling it may be to our pride.

At this Rameses stage of our meditation let us think how glorious has been our deliverance from the Egypt of sin. God delivered the Israelites from their bondage by two means:

First, by price (Isa. xliii. 3; Exod. xv. 13, 16).

Second, by power (Exod. vi. 6, 7; Neh. i. 10).

How vividly this price and this power must have come to the minds of the Israelites when they were assembled in Rameses; for the very name would remind them of the treasure-city they had built in that province, and the awful burdens put upon them (Exod. i. 11).

By the same two means have we been set free: first, by price—and that is Christ (1 Cor. vi. 20, vii. 23); second, by power—and that is Christ's (1 Cor. i. 23, 24; John i. 12).

Notice the beautiful figure in Colossians i. 13, 14: "Who hath delivered us from the power of darkness, and hath translated us into the kingdom of His dear Son: in whom we have redemption through His blood, even the forgiveness of sins." The figure here in Greek is the snatching away of some helpless creature from ruin, even as David rescued the lamb from the hungry lion. Have we not been saved in the same way?

Let us, at the very beginning of this study of the Word, be sure that we have entered upon the journey to the heavenly Canaan by passing through a spiritual Rameses. Fancy some Israelite skulking up into the hills and making a circuit around Beth-shemesh, or going across the river and racing along where the pyramids now stand, in order to join the company of redeemed folk somewhere along in their trip. He might have been received; but it would have been a hard way and an infringement of God's wishes in the matter. But we cannot be truly on the way without going through that experience which Rameses typifies. We must be cleansed before we can be true pilgrims.

Our names may be on the church rolls, but we are not really members of the Lord's host unless we have entered by the station of cleansing. Oh, that the real spirit of David's statement might animate us: "I will wash mine hands in innocency: so will I compass Thine altar, O Lord"! (Ps. xxvi. 6.)

II

SUCCOTH

THE second station of the Israelites in their desert journey was Succoth (Num. xxxiii. 5). "Succoth" means "booths," "tents," or "tabernacles." At this place the Israelites first began to build temporary huts of boughs and branches of trees; hence the naming of the place. Does not all this teach us beautifully that in the Christian's journey from the house of bondage to the Father's house we must be pilgrims? These frail structures, so easily put up and so easily pulled down, represent our beginning to own ourselves loose from the world. Succoth comes rightly after Rameses —as soon as our sins are washed away in the blood of Christ we should begin the life of separateness. Hence from this station we learn these three lessons:

1. *Separation of Christians from the world.*

How constantly is this insisted upon in God's Word! In the very first chapter of the Bible we read that God "divided" the light from the darkness (verse 4), and the waters under the firmament from the waters above the firmament (verse 7). Thus the work was begun, and it has continued ever since. The Greek word *agios*, translated "holy," contains the idea of separation from evil, for it is in this that holiness really consists. The exclusiveness of the Jews in all ages is a type of it. See how God speaks of His separating His chosen people from all other nations in the following passages: Numbers xxiii. 9: "Not reckoned among the nations;" Exodus xxxiii. 16: "So shall we be separated;" Exodus xix. 4: "Brought you unto Myself"—God in His love monopolizing His children. (See also Lev. xx. 24, etc.; 1 Kings viii. 53.)

Christian separation is brought out in that beautiful passage (Cant. iv. 12) where the church is compared to a "garden inclosed" or "barred" (marg.), shut off from the weeds and thistles of the surrounding soil. See also the argument of Peter when the apostles and brethren had come together in the first Christian convention: "To take out of the Gentiles a people for His name" (Acts xv. 14). And in this passage read on a few verses: "To this agree the words of the prophets; . . . I will build again the *tabernacle* of David" —the Succoth idea exactly.

At Succoth the Passover was first observed as a memorial (Exod. xii. 37–50). Now the root idea of the Passover is separation from the world and the blessing that comes with this separation. How fitting that it should first be eaten at Succoth! The Feast of Tabernacles was also instituted to remind the Israelites constantly of their sojourn at Succoth and their separation to God (Lev. xxiii. 33–44). Whenever the streets, courts, and housetops of Jerusalem were filled with the booths of the feast, the people were given a beautiful picture of what God had taught their fathers at Succoth. After the revival described in Nehemiah viii. 1–14, we read that this feast of separation was reëstablished (Neh. viii. 15–17), and the people went out to the mountains to get "boughs and branches of thick trees" to make booths, "*as it is written*"—a very clear reference to the passage before us.

2. *The pilgrimage of Christians.*

We are pilgrims and strangers in this wicked world. The Israelites did not build cities in the desert as if they were to dwell there permanently; they just erected booths that could be easily taken down and removed. Let us, as Christians, be careful not to attach ourselves to the world as if this were our home. Let us seek the city which hath foundations (Heb. xi. 10, 13; 1 Pet. ii. 11–16).

At this our Succoth station we can understand the Book of Leviticus. It is the shortest book of Moses, and to many people the driest book in the Bible. But when we look carefully into it we find it wonderfully instructive. Its key-note is, "Separated unto the Lord." It consists almost entirely of God's own words to His people. It shows God's yearning to draw the Israelites close to His loving heart. They were pilgrims in the desert, and the kind Father would have them feel His presence. This is the honey out of its rock. (See John xvii. 15; 1 Pet. i. 15, 16.) We can also understand 2 Corinthians v. 1. When this body, which is simply the booth or tabernacle in which we live in our desert experience, is taken down, we have a city of permanence to dwell in.

In this view the succeeding verses of the chapter become full of meaning. Hebrews xiii. 13 also becomes plain. Jesus suffered for us outside the gate of Jerusalem. If we truly sympathize with Him "in the fellowship of His sufferings," let us go out to Him in our separated, godly lives, "bearing His reproach." See the striking statement of Judges viii. 16: "He took the elders of the city, and thorns of the wilderness, and briers, and with them he taught the men of Succoth" (marg. says, "Made them to know"). Suffering with Christ makes us to know God, Scripture, self, and sin. Oh, blessed thorns and briers that bring us such knowledge!

3. *God's loving protection of those who separate themselves unto Him.*

Succoth also means "coverings," "protection." Does not this carry a beautiful idea of the Israelites' faith in God? They called a mere temporary booth, swaying in the winds, a protection. The Lord was their preserver, and they were content to dwell in insecure booths. They are well kept whom the Lord keeps.

What glorious promises of protection are given us in the following passages:

Psalm xci. 1: "He that dwelleth in the secret place [or help] of the Most High shall lodge [*sleep at night*] under the shadow of the Almighty." This idea is explained in the Chaldee version of the Scriptures thus: "Under the shadow of the clouds of the glory of the Almighty." (See Matt. xvii. 5; Acts i. 9.)

Isaiah xliii. 2: "When thou passest through the waters, I will be with thee; and through the rivers, they shall not overflow thee: when thou walkest through the fire, thou shalt not be burned." There seems to be a reference here to the crossing of the Red Sea and coming under the scorching sunbeams of the wilderness, from which God defended Israel by the cloud which hovered above them.

Oh, let us go out to God in truly separated lives, and our protection shall be assured! Let us not be afraid of a Christian narrowness conditioned upon the love of Christ. Loyalty to Christ must "press us into narrow limits," in unity of aim and holiness of life (2 Cor. v. 14). Solomon's ideal man is "separated to the search for wisdom" (Prov. xviii. 1). This implies the concentration of the student. Paul's boast was that he was "separated unto the gospel of God" (Rom. i. 1). This implies the noble narrowness, the splendid separateness of the apostle. Thus devoted unto the King, we may boldly claim the King's protection (Heb. xiii. 6).

III

ETHAM

Next to Succoth comes Etham (Num. xxxiii. 6). This was the third stopping-place of the Israelites in the desert. A narrative of what happened to them there is given in Exodus xiii. 20–22. The course, so far, had been a northeasterly one, as may be seen upon maps illustrating the exodus. Etham can be identified with some certainty from the fact mentioned in Exodus that it was "in the edge of the wilderness." The cultivable land at present is probably about as extensive as it was anciently. Hence scholars have located Etham near a place known as the "Seven Wells," about three miles from the western side of the ancient gulf and opposite the head of the gulf.

This was a most trying position to place a people in. They were about to leave a land in which grain would grow and step upon an immense stretch of desert soil. What would they eat in the wilderness? Wherewithal would they be clothed? They were faced by the trial of trust which comes to so many of us at so many periods of life. At Etham they fought the battle out and apparently determined to trust God with a *whole* heart and march forward with an unimpaired confidence; hence, apparently, the naming of the spot.

For Etham means "wholeness" or "perfection." We come at once to the matter of holiness, which is so puzzling to many Christians. Let us see what the Bible says about it. The word "perfection" is used to denote two things in God's Word: (*a*) absolute sinlessness, and (*b*) sincerity.

1. *Perfection we cannot here attain—absolute sinlessness.*

This is a completeness of moral life actually accomplished. This cannot come to us so long as we are in the flesh. Some profess it, but they certainly mistake the teaching of the Word on the subject. Let us study the following points to guide us in the matter:

(*a*) The standard of this perfection (Matt. v. 48; Eph. iv. 13).

(*b*) The Example of this perfection (Heb. ii. 10, v. 8–10, vii. 26–28, marg.). This standard and this Example we should keep constantly before our eyes, and up to them we should strive earnestly, hoping to come as near as possible to them.

(*c*) This perfection not attainable (Rom. viii. 22, 23; Gal. v. 17; 1 John i. 8; Job ix. 20; Luke vi. 40 [though the disciple is perfect, a promise is added]; Mark iv. 28, 29). It seems significant that in Numbers xxxiii. 6 and Exodus xiii. 20, where Etham is mentioned, it is very carefully stated that it was "in the edge of the wilderness." The wilderness of trial, failure, and final success is yet to come.

2. *Perfection we may attain—sincerity.*

The Hebrew word from which "Etham" comes is translated either "perfection" or "sincerity" or "integrity" in the Old Testament. See the following passages, in all of which the word occurs: Genesis xx. 5; 1 Kings ix. 4; Job iv. 6, xxi. 23, marg.; Psalms vii. 8, xxv. 21, xxvi. 1, ci. 2; Isaiah xlvii. 9. Therefore the root idea of the word "Etham," as of holiness, is "wholeness." Cognate words are "heal," "health," "hale." The fundamental idea is completeness or soundness. It is well known that integrity (from *integer*) and sincerity and holiness all mean the same. Indeed, the old English use of the word "perfection" is the same; it means integrity or sincerity. Thomas à Kempis so uses it in his "Imitation of Christ," and St. Augustine says, according to his early English translators, "This is the very perfection of a man, to find out his own imperfection."

Unto this perfection the people came at Etham. They dedicated themselves to a journey of absolute trust in God. They purposed with complete self-surrender to walk with God through the whole desert. They would take bread at His hand, sleep under His protection, and trust Him for water in dry and thirsty lands. That they fell from this consecrated state does not prove that it was at that time insincere. It all is an apt and striking picture of the life of faith as entered upon and prosecuted by the child of God.

Etham comes properly, therefore, after Succoth. When we have had our sins washed away (Rameses), and we have separated ourselves from the world (Succoth), we must walk after God with sincerity. Etham lies at "the *edge* of the wilderness," for we need to have sincerity of purpose at the very start of our divine life.

Pressing toward sinlessness without reserve, coveting

earnestly the spotless character, turning completely from known sin through the power of the Holy Spirit working within us—to all this one may attain and ought to attain. This idea is contained in the following passages: Hebrews vi. 1: "Go on unto" contains metaphor, some think, of a *ship under full sail;* Philippians iii. 12–15: here the two uses of the word "perfect" are contrasted clearly; "not as though already perfect" means absolute sinlessness; "as many as be perfect" (verse 15) means sincerity. In Genesis xxv. 27 it is said, "Jacob was a plain man, dwelling in tents." The word "plain" in Hebrew is *tam*, from which "Etham" comes, and means "perfect." It is so rendered in the Chaldee and other old versions. The meaning is that Jacob had an honest, sincere heart toward God and man—a heart easily read, plain and open, without cloud or covering. The same Hebrew word occurs in the following: Psalm cxix. 1–3, marg.; Genesis vi. 9, marg., xvii. 1, marg.; Job i. 1; Isaiah xlii. 19. Study also the following very significant New Testament passages: 1 Corinthians ii. 6, xiv. 20, marg.; 2 Corinthians vii. 1: "Perfecting holiness," a very remarkable expression, but explained by what has been said above; Matthew xix. 21; 2 Corinthians xiii. 2; James iii. 2.

Etham was distinguished by the wonderful appearance of the pillar of cloud and fire. Up to this point it is said that "God [Elohim] led the people" (Exod. xiii. 17, 18); but now for the first time it is stated that the "Lord [Jehovah] went before them by day in a pillar of cloud, to lead the way; and by night in a pillar of fire, to give them light." This is a most significant change. Elohim is the name of God as Creator—the common Father of us all, saints and sinners alike. Jehovah is the name of God as the Covenant-maker, the Redeemer. In that cloud the "Angel of the covenant," our blessed Saviour, dwelt, and at night His eye of flame shone out. (See Exod. xvi. 10, xl. 34; Num. xvi. 42.) John on Patmos saw the eyes of Jesus to be as "flames of fire" (Rev. i. 14, ii. 18, xix. 12). Out of this cloud our Jesus spoke to Moses and to Israel, and this was the Shechinah, or visible presence, which afterward rested on the most holy place. And it is this glorious presence which, in the last days, shall rest "upon every dwelling-place of Mount Zion" (Isa. iv. 5).

How blessed for us the lesson, therefore, that when we come to our Etham experience and determine to follow the Lord wholly we shall have the pillar always going before us! This will mean to us, as to Israel, three things:

(*a*) Guidance (Exod. xiii. 22; John viii. 12).

(*b*) Protection; from enemies (Exod. xiv. 19); from scorching rays of the sun (Ps. cv. 39; Isa. xxxii. 2; 1 Cor. x. 1; Rom. viii. 28).

(*c*) Encouragement (Exod. xiv. 14; John xiv. 16).

In 1 Corinthians xiii. 10 the word "perfect" is used to denote our Lord in His second coming, at which time charity shall be manifested, and the Christian shall know perfectly (with wholeness), and not in part. Then Christ shall say of saintly character, as He said of His atonement on the dark day, "It is perfected" (John xix. 30).

The perfection to which we may here attain is very

well expressed in the word "blamelessness." The child who tries his best to please is blameless, though what he does may not be faultless. (See Phil. ii. 15, iii. 6; 1 Thess. v. 23; 2 Pet. iii. 14; 1 Cor. i. 8; 1 Tim. iii. 10.)

The perfection to which we shall attain only when the waters of death have purged us utterly is "faultlessness." We may be "kept from falling" in the present life, but we shall be "faultless" only when we are "presented before the presence of His glory with exceeding joy" (Jude 24).

IV

PI-HAHIROTH

By direct command of God the Israelites were turned from the northeasterly course they had been taking, which was the direct route to Palestine, and caused to bend down to the southward (Exod. xiv. 2). This took them round the foot-hills and mountains of Beth-shemesh, and led them toward the upper arm of the Red Sea. This change of course was probably reported to Pharaoh, and led him to hope that the Israelites, by their backward movement, would entangle themselves as in a net. Deeper and deeper would they thus plunge themselves into the unknown wilderness, and thus they might fall an easy prey to his armies (Exod. xiv. 3, 4). It may have been also that this determined push toward the depths of the desert brought to Pharaoh his first realization that his slaves had really "fled" (verse 5). Up to this time he may have consoled himself with the reflection that the people had gone for a few days to offer sacrifice. Now he knew they were determined to escape him entirely and forever.

Hastily he gathered his army, the principal strength of which lay in his "six hundred chosen chariots."

Pictures of such chariots are common upon the Egyptian monuments—the two fiery war-horses, the two warriors in each chariot, one driving and holding only a shield for personal defense, and the other fully armed and devoting his whole attention to active assault. Such a force would be extremely formidable to this fleeing mass of people untrained at arms, encumbered by women and children, flocks and herds, and whom long years of slavery had tended to weaken and dispirit. It is hardly to be wondered at that they "murmured" in despair and affright. Escape was cut off in every direction. Eastward was the sea; to the west and south the mountains stood sheer and forbidding. They could see the rays of the setting sun glinting on the Egyptian war-chariots bearing down upon them from the northward. What were they to do?

The story of God's gracious deliverance of them is a familiar one. Study the fourteenth chapter of Exodus to get the full picture. First, God commanded silence and trust. Even prayer was out of order: "Wherefore criest thou unto Me?" Jehovah "looked" with blazing eye upon the Egyptians out of the pillar of fire. His anger was hot and burning. The next day "Jehovah shook off the Egyptians in the midst of the sea" (Exod. xiv. 27, marg.).

The night before this wondrous deliverance God would have the people encamp at Pi-hahiroth. They must sleep in the very presence of their danger; their trust in God must be tested in the silent watches of the night. God did His part by putting a barrier between them and their enemies (verse 20), and the people learned their lesson and grew calm. The very meaning of "Pi-hahiroth" teaches us this, for it signifies "liberties" or "escapes." On that encampment fell the peace of an assured escape from Pharaoh and his hosts on the morrow.

Many Old Testament passages use this incident as an illustration of spiritual escape, and in the New Testament it is referred to as a type of Christian liberty. As soon as we leave the Etham stage, on our way to the heavenly Canaan, we are very apt to be overtaken by enemies. When once we determine to follow Christ with a perfect heart we are assailed by those who would "beguile us of our reward"; but if we are obedient and faithful to the commands of our Lord we are given a glorious escape into a land of true liberty. Notice four general points:

1. *What is Christian liberty?*

The fifth chapter of Galatians gives it all to us in a nutshell, telling us what it is not and what it is.

(*a*) It is not legalism (verses 1–6). (See John viii. 32.)

(*b*) It is not leisure (verses 7–12). (See James i. 25, ii. 12.)

(*c*) It is not license (verse 13). (See 1 Pet. ii. 16; Rom. vi. 7, etc.) "A free man is one who does not what he pleases, but what he ought."

(*a*) It is love (verses 14–17). (See Rom v. 15–21.)

(*b*) It is leading (verses 18–24). (See 2 Cor. iii. 17.)

(*c*) It is life (verses 25, 26). (See Rom. viii. 1, 2, 21.)

2. *How do we attain Christian liberty?*

The Israelites came to Pi-hahiroth through Etham. How are we set free from sin? Not as slaves were liberated in Exodus xxi. 26, 27, by the passing of years and calamities. We escape by accepting, with a sincere and unreserved heart, the truth as it is in Christ (John viii. 32–36; Gal. v. 1). Hence result these two duties: activity as doers of the Word (James i. 25) and abiding in our calling with assured trust in God (1 Cor. vii. 21–23).

3. *From what are we freed?*

The Israelites escaped seven things at Pi-hahiroth, and we are saved from the same.

(*a*) Fear (Exod. xiv. 13; Rom. viii. 15; Luke v. 10). (See all the "fear nots" of Christ.)

(*b*) Working (Exod. xiv. 14; Rom. iv. 4, 5; Matt. xiv. 28–31).

(*c*) Darkness (Exod. xiv. 20; Col. i. 3; 2 Cor. iii. 17, 18).

(*d*) Law. Israelites had freedom from natural law (Exod. xiv. 29), we from law of sin (1 Cor. xv. 56, 57).

(*e*) Sin (Exod. xiv. 31; Rom. vi. 18, viii. 21).

(*f*) Death (Exod. xv. 2; Hos. xiii. 14; Rom. viii. 37).

(*g*) Judgment (Exod. xv. 13; John v. 24: "Shall not come into *judgment*." This word, translated "condemnation," is the same in the Greek as that rendered "judgment" in verses 22 and 27).

4. *The dangers of liberty.*

The liberty of the Christian is a glorious thing, but it involves certain dangers. The Israelites at Pi-hahiroth murmured against God (Exod. xiv. 11) and fell into pride (Exod. xiv. 12). Thus there is danger of our liberty running into license (1 Pet. ii. 16; Gal. v. 13; James ii. 12; 1 Cor. vi. 12, 13, viii. 9).

It is a blessed thing that in Christ we are free from fear of men and fear of conscience and fear of judgment, but we are not free from fear of God. We are free from working *for* our salvation, but we are not free from working *out* our salvation. We are free from darkness, but not from light; from law, but not from grace; from sin, but not from service. We are free from death, but we are crucified to the world. Our commission is not "Do and live," but "Live and do."

When their deliverance had been accomplished, Moses and all the children of Israel sang a song of jubilee (Exod. xv. 1-19). And Miriam took up the strain, and all the women followed her out with timbrels and with dances. What a stirring picture is this of the praise of the church universal on earth, as well as the church triumphant in heaven! Every Sabbath this song of thanksgiving was repeated in the Jewish temple when the drink-offering was poured out. Thus God reminded Israel that to all time His kingdom shall be surrounded by the hostile powers of this world, that there shall always be contest between them, but that He will surely interpose to save His people and destroy their enemies. What a comfort all this is to us, and what a prophecy of final and complete victory! The day is coming when they who stand on the "sea of glass," who have "gotten the victory" and have the "harps of God," shall sing "the song of Moses the servant of God, and the song of the Lamb." Oh, that we may have a part in that song of thanksgiving for the *escapes* God has given us in the desert!

In Isaiah lxi. 1, 2, we have our mission. In Ezekiel xlvi. 16, 17, we have our warning; for at our day of jubilee, if the gift of life is to continue with us forever, we must be *sons*, and not mere *servants*.

V

MARAH

ONE of the most significant verses of this chapter we are considering, the thirty-third of Numbers, is the eighth: "And they departed from before Pi-hahiroth, and passed through the midst of the sea into the wilderness, and went three days' journey in the wilderness of Etham, and pitched in Marah." Here are many thoughts of value to us in our Christian training. The words "journey," "wilderness," "through the midst of the sea," are very common in our hymns and homilies. Most of all is the word "Marah" used. Every one knows that "Marah" means "bitterness," and sooner or later every one of us must pitch beside its waters, that sting so upon the lips and taste so like gall in the throat.

The circumstance that the Israelites passed through the sea to Marah is used by St. Paul (1 Cor. x. 2) to teach an important spiritual lesson. They "were all baptized unto Moses in the cloud and in the sea." It is a picture of absolute feebleness offered in complete subjection to the divine power as shown His servant. It typifies the baptism of submission by which we are weaned from and cut off from the pomp and pleasures of this world. We die unto Egypt with all its splendors and delights. We are made disciples to the divine light by means of trials and afflictions.

What befell the people at Marah is told us in Exodus xv. 22–26. It is a very vivid narrative. The moment they pass through the sea they find their feet upon desert soil. Hardships begin, continue, and multiply. For three days they press forward through the briers and over the rocks; there is no water for them to drink, and they, with their beasts, begin to suffer. With an eagerness which has often been shown in similar circumstance they rush to the brink of certain wells whose fringing palms appear upon the horizon. Alas, the waters are brackish and bitter! Neglected, the wells have filled with alkali and rubbish. The sight of the water which cannot be used only intensifies the awful thirst which the three days' march through the dusty desert has produced.

The people murmur. Moses prays, and then a miracle is performed. The waters are sweetened. Then God proves the people and makes for them "a statute and an ordinance." He improves every occasion to teach great lessons and lead those under instruction to full surrender to Himself. He adds a promise (verse 26) of immunity from the diseases which had been brought upon the Egyptians, and pledges Himself to be their healer. God gives a commentary upon this through the mouth of Jeremiah (xxx. 11): "I will correct thee in measure, and will not leave thee altogether unpunished." Yet the meaning is, the result of this discipline shall be spiritual healing. The people had tested God as Jehovah "the Redeemer" and Jehovah "a Man of war," and now they were to find Him "Jehovah-rophi," "the Lord that healeth thee."

The very common use of Marah as a type of spiritual experience justifies the use of all the other stations of the desert for purposes of instruction. Under the Spirit's direction we may here find all the experiences of the Christian life illustrated and unfolded. Marah may come to us very early in life, as it came to Israel as the fifth station on the way. Or we may come to its bitter waters just before we reach the Jordan at the end of our earthly pilgrimage. Or we may have something of its bitterness in our cups for long periods together. Let us try to grasp its lessons at once, and so be benefited by its teachings whenever we stoop at its brink.

Let us consider:

1. *The prevalence of affliction.*

Marah comes immediately after Pi-hahiroth. Thus does sorrow travel upon the heels of joy. Only three days after the Israelites had sung in triumph under the leadership of Moses and Miriam we find them murmuring beside the bitter well. Our Lord was led from His baptism at the Jordan into the wilderness to be tempted of the devil. So does it often happen that sorrow and trial come immediately after moments of exaltation and victory. Look at three passages which illustrate the prevalence of affliction: Ezekiel ix. 4; Genesis xvi. 6–8 (another scene in the wilderness of Shur, where Marah stood); Ruth i. 20. And then look at the Bible names, Mary, Miriam, Merari, Meraiah, Merioth, Imrah; the meaning of all these words is "bitterness," for they are all derived from the word

"Marah." Almost every page in the Bible teaches us the prevalence of sorrow in the world.

2. *The waters sweetened.*

The bitter well at Marah was sweetened by casting a tree into it. This tree was a type of Christ, the Branch, ready to fall, if so be the hearts of His people might be sweetened (Zech. vi. 12, 13). Oh, if it were not for the power of the Branch, which turns all our defeats into glorious victories, we should be miserable indeed! As Trapp says, this tree is a "type of Christ's sweet cross and easy yoke, that sweeteneth and facilitateth all our light afflictions." The Jewish doctors say that this tree was itself bitter, and add this note: "It is the manner of the blessed God to sweeten that which is bitter by that which is bitter."

In John ii. 11 it is said that Christ "manifested forth His glory" by changing water into wine. Now water signifies "sorrow" in the Bible, and wine is the type of joy. It is, indeed, Christ's glory to change sorrow into joy and death into life. (See also Isa. xi. 1–4, 10; Hos. ii. 15.) Paul knew how the bitter waters of life are to be sweetened. (See Phil. iv. 11–13.)

3. *The use of afflictions.*

It will be found useful to look up the following passages, in each of which the Hebrew root from which the word "Marah" comes occurs in one form or another. We will see how important this desert station is to God's people, and also how it should be used (2 Kings xiv. 26; Prov. xiv. 10; Gen. xxvi. 35, marg.; Isa. lviii. 7, marg.; Lam. i. 7, iii. 19. See also Heb. xii. 7, 8: our sonship is shown by our afflictions; 2

Cor. iv. 17: here we have a series of contrasts between "light" and "weight," "affliction" and "glory," "a moment" and "eternal").

4. *How to bear afflictions.*
Psalm lv. 22: Roll thy burden upon the Lord.
Psalm xxxvii. 5, marg.: Roll thy way upon the Lord.
Proverbs xvi. 3, marg.: Roll thy works upon the Lord.
Psalm xxii. 8, marg.: Roll thyself upon the Lord.
Then afflictions will be light burdens and easy yokes.

VI

ELIM

How sudden and complete are the changes in the experiences of the Israelites! In one verse we find them at Pi-hahiroth, in the next verse they are at Marah, and now they have come to Elim, where "were twelve fountains of water, and threescore and ten palm-trees" (Num. xxxiii. 9). The verses which describe this event are simple, but very suggestive. They are striking examples of the style of writing God employs. If mere uninspired men had written the Bible we should have had a wonderful account of Elim, with its fountains and groves of palms. The approach of the people to its rest and shade would have been minutely described. God writes not so; He tells us enough to strengthen faith, but adds nothing as a stimulant to curiosity. The "wells" and "trees" are mentioned both in Exodus (xv. 27) and in Numbers. The pitching of the tents and the remaining in encampment until man and beast have enjoyed a strengthening and much-needed rest are hinted at; more than this God does not think it worth while to describe. Elim may mean two things: either "strengths" or "God's strong angels." And the sudden coming to this beautiful place of refreshment is a surprise to us. But is not just this every Christian's experience? Does God leave us long at Marah? Does He not rather lead us speedily to Elim, if we trust Him, where fountains of spiritual refreshment are? These abrupt changes in the desert experiences of the Israelites show us how accurately their journeys prefigure the several phases of the Christian life.

What lessons may we learn at our Elim, our places of joy and strength in life's desert?

1. *We should learn that after the baptism of suffering comes the dispensation of strength.*

If God leads us to Marah, where we are called upon to suffer, He does it because this is the right road to Elim, where we are made strong in His service. See how this idea is brought out in the following Old Testament passages: Isaiah xxvi. 1–4, xl. 29–31. The New Testament is also full of promises of divine strength to those who trust. Study carefully 2 Corinthians xii. 9: "My strength is made perfect." It may be that Paul had Elim in mind when he wrote this verse, for he uses a verb in the last clause drawn from camping experiences: "Most gladly, . . . that the power of Christ may spread its tabernacle or pavilion over me." See also Hebrews xii. 11: when we are at the Marah of suffering let us try to think of this "afterward," when the "peaceable fruit of righteousness" shall drop from the palm-trees of Elim.

It is the special and blessed work of Christ to lead His children from sorrow to joy. In Hebrews ii. 16, marg., it is said of Him that He "taketh not hold" of angels, but of the seed of Abraham. This same word is used in Matthew xiv. 31, where Christ "took hold" of Peter, and drew him out of the water. Our hold upon Christ may be very weak,—as weak as Peter's faith,—but His hold upon us can never be broken. How beautiful, therefore, is the conclusion in Hebrews ii. 18: "He Himself has suffered, and so is able to help [and hold] those who are tempted"! The prophecy in regard to Him in Isaiah lxi. 3 brings out this idea also; for it is said that the mourning ones shall "be called trees [i.e., "strengths," for the word is "Elim"] of righteousness, The planting of the Lord, that He might be glorified."

A great deal is said of our hold upon Christ (i.e., our faith in Him), but not enough about *His strong hold on us.* The passage in Hebrews referred to above (ii. 18) contains a Greek word (*epilambano*) that is most significant. It implies a strong hand and true, backed by a loving heart and expressed in a firm grasp. The same word is used in the following: Mark viii. 23; Luke ix. 47, xiv. 4, xx. 20, 26, xxiii. 26; Acts ix. 27, xvi. 19, xvii. 19, xviii. 17, xxi. 30, 33, xxiii. 19; 1 Timothy vi. 12, 19; Hebrews viii. 9.

So when Christ "takes hold" of us there is no danger that the grasp will slip. And be assured of three things:

(*a*) Rescue from the guilt of sin (Rom. v. 7–9).

(*b*) Rescue from the power and love of sin (Rom. v. 10).

(*c*) Rescue from even the bodily consequences of sin at Christ's coming (Rom. viii. 23; Heb. ix. 28).

2. *The ministry of the angels is to refresh after conflict.*

Elim also means "God's strong angels." What is the office of the angels? It is to refresh and strengthen after the Marahs of conflict have been passed. They are the ministering spirits to help on the travelers to the good land. In all the following passages this idea is brought out: Genesis xxi. 15-19, xxxii. 1, 2; 1 Kings xix. 5-8; Daniel x. 16-19; Matthew iv. 11; Hebrews i. 14; Luke xv. 10, xvi. 22.

The Jews believe that the seventy palm-trees at Elim were typical of the seventy angels who attend the throne of God, and that they also represented the seventy elders comprising the sanhedrim. These numbers are supposed to show the "strength" of these two bodies—the angels in their support of God's works and the sanhedrim in the support of the Jewish nation. We are also reminded of the seventy disciples whom the Lord sent forth (Luke x. 1) to "strengthen" the early church at the beginning of its Christian journey.

The twelve fountains may represent to us the refreshment afforded by the Holy Spirit to the *whole* church. Twelve was the Jewish sign of completeness, being the number of the tribes of Israel. The twelve apostles are undoubtedly designed to represent also the completeness of instruction and blessing prepared for the Christian church. There is not a disposition of mind that will not be met, not a willing heart that cannot be satisfied. The poorest and weakest of the Lord's brethren may come and drink freely at Elim. Not one need be left out. Not one need miss the strength and refreshment which the angels are prepared to administer to us after our sorrows and conflicts.

VII

RED SEA

THERE is something pathetic in the record that the Israelites were compelled to leave Elim, and turn back or aside to the Red Sea (Num. xxxiii. 10). The ninth verse tells us that they had "pitched" their tents at Elim, as if they had hoped to have a resting-space of some length under the seventy palms and beside the twelve cooling fountains. But this place of enjoyment and privilege was not good for them. They began to be puffed up with pride and to forget what God had done for them. So they are led back to the Red Sea, that the sight of its waves might flash upon their minds a remembrance of the glorious deliverance God had given them there from the Egyptians. In the Hebrew the name "Red Sea" signifies the "sea of entanglements" or the "sea of destruction." And often does God lead Christians a little way back upon their journey to show them what He has done for them by way of bringing them out of destruction and through entanglements.

By looking at the map in your Bibles showing the peninsula of Sinai, you will see that the course of the Israelites had been southeasterly through the desert of

Etham to Marah and Elim. You will observe that the mountains seem to close up farther progress in that direction, and that thus they were forced to turn aside and come close to the sea whose shores they had in a general way, though at a distance, been following. God used that spur of hills to accomplish His loving purposes; so it is with us. He uses nature, society, material things,—*all* things,—to bring us to remembrance of His spiritual mercies. Sometimes He closes up our way in business or shuts us up in our homes with sickness to turn our minds back to the entanglements out of which He has delivered us. "Come ye aside into the desert place and rest awhile." "Come ye to the Red Sea and think awhile." Thus our God speaks to us.

Let us take our Bibles and study these two things:

1. *Our tendency to forget what God has done for us.*

It is amazing that the Israelites could ever allow that awful scene at the Red Sea, when the Egyptians were destroyed, to pass from their minds. Yet they did; and how frequently God caused the psalmists and prophets to speak of it in order to renew their remembrance! Look at Psalm cxxxvi. 13-15; Numbers xxi. 14; Deuteronomy xi. 4; Joshua ii. 10; Nehemiah ix. 9; Psalm cvi. 9; Jeremiah xlix. 21. In all these passages God appeals to His people to remember what He did for them at the Red Sea.

But are we any the less forgetful? How frequently do our Lord and the apostles call upon us to remember! (See Matt. xvi. 9; Luke xvi. 25, xvii. 32, xxiv. 6; John xv. 20; Acts xx. 31, 35; Eph. ii. 11; 2 Tim. ii. 8; Jude 17.) When Charles I. was on the scaffold he lifted up his finger and said to his enemies, who clustered around him, "Remember!" With how much greater pathos does our Lord speak to us in this time, when so much needs to be done for Christ, to remember the past, from which we have been saved, the present, in which we might accomplish so much, and the future, to which we hasten!

2. *God's method of bringing us to remembrance.*

God did not preach a sermon to the Israelites; He just led them back to the Red Sea that they might see the place where He had delivered them; and after this, when Moses was giving his final directions to the Israelites, he tells them to go back to the Red Sea, that a sight of that familiar spot might call them to repentance of their sins (Deut. i. 40). This sea received its name from the *bulrushes* that grew in it, and hence, being called the "sea of entanglements" or "destruction," it would bring to the Israelites a vivid idea of the spiritual entanglements into which they had fallen, as well as the destruction of their enemies. In the same way does God use the association of ideas to bring us to repentance.

We should particularly remember our redemption through Christ. This was typified in the deliverance through the Red Sea. Study carefully Acts vii. 36, 37, where Stephen uses it as an illustration of Christ's blood, burial, and resurrection.

John iii. 16: God's part in redemption—*love.*

1 Peter i. 18, 19: Christ's part in redemption—*blood.*

John xvi. 8–11: The Holy Spirit's part in redemption—*application.*

We should also remember God's delivering providences:

Psalm lvi. 13: Deliverance from spiritual *death*.
Daniel vi. 22: Deliverance from *temptation*.
Psalm lvi. 8–10: Deliverance from *affliction*.

Ah, it is well for us to turn back now and again to see these greedy Egyptians from whom God has delivered us!

For a beautiful illustration of how God uses the association of ideas to call us to repentance, study John xxi. 4–13. Peter had denied the Lord, and Christ wished to reinstate him. To do this He appears to him when Peter had been fishing and had caught nothing. How vividly would this recall to the apostle's mind the circumstances under which Christ had first called him unto His service! (See Matt. iv. 18, 19.) And as Peter had denied the Lord three times, and beside a fire of coals (John xviii. 18), so did Christ have a fire of coals on the shore, and require Peter to testify thrice to his love for the Master.

Another example of God's use of old memories to stir up new purposes and resolves we have in the story of Joseph and his brethren (Gen. xlii. 7–18). Joseph spake roughly to the brethren, accused them of being spies, put them into prison, and bound Simeon before their eyes. These things would vividly recall to them the rough speaking they had been guilty of to the little lad years before, the accusations heaped upon the "dreamer," the cruelties practised, and the final plunging of him into the pit. That old scene in Dothan was reënacted in all its essential features in Egypt, and thus God brought the brethren of Joseph to repentance.

Then there is the story of the widow of Zarephath (1 Kings xvii. 17, 18). When the woman's son fell sick she burst into the presence of the prophet and cried, "Art thou come unto me to call my sin to remembrance?" She had tried to hide that old sin, to forget it. But there is, now and then, an awful awakening of memory. The coming of the prophet had something in it to bring the old scenes back — scenes out of which all the pleasure had faded and only the pain remained. Oh, how often God uses memory to draw from parched lips the agonizing confession, "I have sinned"!

VIII

WILDERNESS OF SIN

GETTING under way again after their swerving to the Red Sea, we find the Israelites in the wilderness of Sin (Num. xxxiii. 11). They go around the rocky promontory which brought them to the water's edge, and then they are able to leave the sea and pursue their inland journey. A defile in the mountains opens up a way for them. (See map of peninsula of Sinai.) It is a hard climb, and there are many discomforts. They will be entangled in the mountains all the way until they get over to Hazeroth. Pasturage is scanty, food is hard to get, water is scarce. There are bushes to trip their feet and briers to pierce their flesh, and any number of confusing valleys to make them lose their way and their tempers. It is a very trying portion of the way; but it had lessons for them and has many lessons for us.

"Sin" in the Hebrew signifies "a bramble" or "enmity"; and judging from the experiences of the Israelites in this desert, it was very appropriately named. Read carefully the sixteenth chapter of Exodus to see what befell them there. Spiritually this station signifies to us a state of discontent, when enmity, like a bramble, lacerates the heart and induces us to murmur against providence. It was common among the Hebrews to speak of rebellious people as "briers" or "brambles." (See Ezek. ii. 6.) Notice:

1. *The rise of enmity against God.*

In the wilderness of Sin the Israelites revealed that they possessed those carnal hearts which are enmity against God (Rom. viii. 7). They clung to the friendship of the world, which is enmity with God (James iv. 4). They had just been at Elim, where were the fountains and palm-trees, and would soon be at Sinai, where the law would be given. Yet they became discontented and murmured (Exod. xvi. 2, 3). Man's first temptation was to discontent (Gen. iii. 1), and his evil affections have always been like brambles to set him in enmity against God (Isa. xxvii. 4). Israel murmured thirteen times in the wilderness (Exod. v. 21, xiv. 10, xv. 24, xvi. 2, xvii. 2, xxxii. 1; Num. xi. 1, 4, xii. 1, xiv. 2, xvi. 3, xx. 2, xxi. 5); but the later Jews were not a whit better, for they murmured precisely under the same circumstances, i.e., when bread was promised (John vi. 41–43).

The root of the discontent of Israel was worldliness. The people hungered for the flesh-pots of Egypt; and the secret of modern Christian discontent and distrust is the same. It is not only painful but pitiable to hear God's children murmuring against their lot, for it shows that their hearts are fixed upon worldly things. Oh, that the disciple might be willing to be as his Lord! Oh, that every Christian might bear in mind Christ's warning, "Remember Lot's wife!" Some scholars say that the Greek word translated "holy" in the New Testament is a compound of two other words, meaning literally "without the world." Would that we all were holy in this sense!

2. *God's cure of enmity.*

Manna was given from heaven to cure the enmity of Israel (Exod. xvi. 4). In like manner Christ, the Bread from heaven, was sent to "abolish in His flesh the enmity" of man toward God (Eph. ii. 15). See how gloriously two passages, Genesis iii. 15, and Ephesians ii. 16, link the opening and the closing of the Bible together.

Probably the best meaning of the word "manna" is "numbered" or "prepared." The idea is that God tenderly computed the needs of His children, and lovingly prepared the right means to satisfy them. In the same way does He cure Christian discontent. He does not argue with us or berate us; He goes on patiently to supply our wants; He feeds us with Christ. For every day He supplies a daily portion (2 Kings xxv. 30). At last His goodness leads us to repentance, and we learn that the very hairs of our heads are "numbered," and that our sustenance is sure. Study carefully John vi. 31–59. See also how Christ is prefigured in Psalm lxxviii. 25. And since Christ is our refreshment, let us gladly obey the invitation of Canticles v. 1.

This sixteenth chapter of Exodus gives us a beautiful comparison between the manna and Christ, the true Bread from heaven.

1. Both were despised (verse 14).
2. Both were rejected (verse 15).
3. Both were proclaimed (verse 15).

4. Both were then accepted (verse 18).

5. Both were discovered to be altogether lovely (verse 31).

6. Benefits of both may be handed down to our children (verse 32).

7. Refreshment derived from both is sufficient for the whole journey unto Canaan (verse 35).

Take notice how Paul draws detailed lessons for us from the whole story of the wilderness of Sin (1 Cor. x. 3–11). Let the bramble of strict self-examination pierce each one of us, that we make no mistake. Hawthorne tells of a prisoner who, having been liberated from a long service in jail, returns to his childhood home and there plucks a rose, crushing it with its thorn in his hand to convince himself that he is not dreaming. The pain in his palm was a proof to him of the reality of his return. So may the prick of conscience or the deep piercing of affliction show that we are sons of God, and that we have been liberated from the bondage to sin. "Whom the Lord loveth He chasteneth."

IX

DOPHKAH

PURSUING their way along one of the wadies of the wilderness of Sin, the people come to a station called Dophkah (Num. xxxiii. 12). This defile has been identified by modern travelers as what is now known as the wadi Maghara. It is a wide valley shut in by barren hills, highly colored and most picturesque and beautiful, but for the most part devoid of vegetation. Immediately around Dophkah there seems to have been some softening of the desert barrenness, for the record is, "They took their journey out of the wilderness of Sin." There was more pasturage and a certain supply of water, though neither could have been very abundant. For the last few days they had been pursuing the most trying and difficult part of their journey; their sufferings from the heat and dust and lack of water, which had been intense in Shur and Etham, became almost intolerable in the fastnesses of the wilderness of Sin. The walls of rock on each side of them greatly intensified the heat by reflection of the sun's rays. The great company which had made such a sublime picture at the first, marching out with banners and tents, flocks and herds, groups of horsemen and troops of joyous children, had now become a bedraggled, weary, woebegone procession with scarcely the ability to drag one foot after the other.

The experience of a traveler along this route has recently been described as follows: "At dawn the day is mild and balmy as an Italian spring, and inconceivably lovely in the colors shed on earth, air, and sky; but presently the sun bursts up from the sea, a fierce enemy that will force every one to crouch before him. For two hours his rays are endurable, but after that they become a fiery ordeal. The morning beams oppress you with a feeling of sickness; their steady glow blinds your eyes, blisters your skin, and parches your mouth, till you have only one thought — when evening is to come. At noon the heat, reverberated by the glowing hills, is like the blast of a lime-kiln. The wind sleeps on the reeking shore; the sky is dead white. Men are not so much sleeping as half senseless; they feel as if a few more degrees of heat would be death."

It is hardly to be wondered at that the people were more than ever discouraged "because of the way." The terrific heat, the empty water-skins, the stiff climb, the uncertainty as to any adequate supply of water to wash their manna down, all conspired to discourage them. Suddenly they come to Dophkah, where an unexpected mercy meets them to relieve their minds and inspirit them for the farther journey. This mercy was not the giving of an abundance of water out of a rock; it was not even the finding of wells or fountains such as had cheered them at Elim. Some water-supply was there, as has been said, because there were several hundred people living permanently at Dophkah. God granted the Israelites a mercy higher even than the giving of water to drink. It was an appeal to their better natures on the part of God, a "knocking at their hearts" of a subtler and more blessed character.

Dophkah means "knocking," as at a door. The significance of the name is not far to seek. We know, as a matter of history and by inscriptions legible at the present day, that in this part of the mountains were extensive mines of copper and turquoise. For centuries these mines had been worked, the Egyptians sending hither their political prisoners. It was a place of penal servitude, as Siberia is at the present day. There were noblemen and slaves, the innocent and guilty, men, women, and children, all driven to their underground tasks by cruel overseers. Seven hundred and fifty soldiers guarded the entrances of the mines to see that none escaped. Death was the only release. Among the slaves and prisoners were many Israelites, brethren and friends of the people who now came marching to Dophkah. Dr. Georg Ebers supposes that Joshua was one of these captives.

What a glad surprise it was, not only to the Hebrew slaves in the mines but also to the liberators, when God led Moses and his host this way to free the captives! What embraces, tears, family reunions, there must have been! That an actual release was accomplished is implied even by the inscriptions on the rocks around the place. Though the mines were unexhausted and are rich to this day, the inscriptions show that the work was suddenly stopped. The machinery even was found in its place, left by those who were brought out so suddenly. Thus God "knocked" at the hearts of Israel. Through this signal mercy did He seek to reach the captive spirits toiling in misery away down in the darkness of sin. Thus did He desire, and thus does He always desire, to bring poor struggling souls up into His own sunshine and peace.

In the Scriptures "knocking" is used in two ways: man may knock or God may knock. The root from which the word "Dophkah" comes is used in the Song of Solomon v. 2: "It is the voice of my beloved that *knocketh*." This is the only place in the Old Testament where the figure is used; but it is common in the New Testament. Here, in this thought of tender pleading, is one of the differences between the old dispensation and this in which we live. There are three knocks and three answers spoken of in the Bible:

1. *Man's timely knock for mercy—the door always opened.*

Among the first promises the Christ made to man is this: "To him that knocketh it shall be opened" (Matt. vii. 7, 8). Again, He says that He will in nowise cast out the poorest supplicant (John vi. 37). The Italian version renders this, "I will in nowise thrust him out of doors." The figure is of a poor man who knocks at a rich man's door praying for bread. The bread is always given. Let the sinner, therefore, knock earnestly with prayer, taking Christ as an example in this as in everything (Heb. v. 7).

2. *Christ's knock at man's heart—the door sometimes opened.*

What a beautiful picture do we have in the Song of Solomon v. 2, and how is this carried out in the sublime declaration of Revelation iii. 20. Happy is the man who opens his heart to Christ. See how the apostle in Ephesians iii. 19 glories in the fullness that Christ gives to the soul. At Dophkah the Israelites opened their hearts in penitence to the knocking mercies of God, and they supped with Him upon the manna He had prepared. How complete is the parallelism between this scene and Revelation iii. 20! Christ knocks, and if we open our hearts He comes in, sits down with us, and sups with us upon a feast of manna which He has provided. That manna is Himself (1 Cor. x. 3, 4; Rev. ii. 17).

Read the whole of the fifth chapter of the Song of Solomon. In striking orientalism the entire picture of Christ's pleading with the sinner is presented. He "knocks," He "calls," He puts His hand in "at the hole of the door." Then what gladness is shown in the fifth verse: "I rose up to open to my beloved; and my hands dropped with myrrh, and my fingers with sweet-smelling myrrh, upon the handles of the lock." The myrrh is a type of sacrifice, and so when we open to Christ we are prepared to give up all for Him. Myrrh is the type of all sweetness and satisfaction coming through sacrifice. These will be ours, and to the last we will be able to say, "He is altogether lovely. This is my beloved, and this is my friend, O daughters of Jerusalem" (v. 16).

3. *Man's untimely knock for mercy—the door never opened.*

Let all the careless study these passages: Matthew vii. 21-23, xxv. 10-13; Luke xiii. 24-28; Hebrews iii. 18, 19; Proverbs i. 24-28.

There is one passage in which the word "Dophkah" occurs which is of the greatest practical import. It is Judges xix. 22. Here we behold the sons of Belial "besetting the house round about and beating at the door." Their purposes were evil and their hearts were full of sin. What a type do they present of man's natural inclinations! Let the aim of all Christian workers be to lead poor blinded men to the door of mercy, where, if they knock, the Lord will open to them and give them peace. To save men is the only thing worth staying an hour out of heaven for.

X

ALUSH

AFTER a period of rest in Dophkah the Israelites took their journey still farther into the fastnesses of the mountains and encamped in Alush (Num. xxxiii. 13). Doubtless it would have been pleasant for them to remain long before the emptied mines, but this was not God's plan. Time enough was probably allowed for the rescued captives to regain something of their former strength under the influences of hope and friendship, as well as by means of proper food and the fresh air of heaven. Around the tent doors semicircles would be formed at evening, and the stories of hardships and oppression would be recounted. Nothing revives as hope and love do. A difference soon became apparent upon the faces and in the walk and actions of the captives; and then God, through Moses, gave the command to go forward. Too long rest at Dophkah would produce either arrogance or inertness. It was above all things necessary to keep the people on the move. God's great mercies, "knocking" at their hearts, must have time to enter. Then the people must up and take the path again. The wadi still climbs upward. The way is toward deeper solitude of barren mountains; and just beyond Alush is the wide valley overrun by the fierce Amalekites.

On the way from Dophkah to Alush, we are told, the first glorious view of Sinai bursts upon the traveler. Ebers describes the scene on the afternoon when the Israelites came to the spot.

"Men, women, and children all fixed their eyes and pointed with hands, sticks, and crooks to the same spot, for there, before them, a strange and novel spectacle attracted their gaze. A shout of amazement and delight broke from their parched and weary lips, which had long ceased to stir for speech; it rapidly spread from one division to the next, from tribe to tribe, to the lepers that closed the train and the vanguard beyond. One and another elbowed his neighbor and whispered a name familiar to them all — that of the holy mountain, where the Lord had promised to Moses that He would lead His people into a good and pleasant land flowing with milk and honey. None had told the weary multitude that this was the place, and yet they knew that they beheld Horeb and the peak of Sinai, the most sacred summit of this mass of granite. Although but a mountain, yet it was the throne of the Almighty God of their fathers.

"At this hour the whole sacred hill seemed, like the burning bush out of which He had there spoken to His chosen servant, to be steeped in fire. Its seven-peaked crown towered from afar, high above the hills and vales that surrounded it, burning like an enormous ruby lighted up by a blaze of glory in the clouds.

"Such a sight none of them had ever beheld. But the sun sank lower and lower and disappeared in the sea, which the mountain hid from their view; the glowing ruby turned to solemn amethyst and then to the deep purple of the violet; but the people still gazed spellbound on the holy mount. Nay, even when the day-star had altogether vanished, and only its reflection bordered the edge of a long, level cloud with gleaming gold, they opened their eyes the wider, for a man of the tribe of Benjamin, his brain turned by the splendor of the scene, declared that they beheld the trailing mantle of Jehovah, and those about him to whom he pointed it out caught the pious rapture.

"For a little while the pilgrims had forgotten thirst and exhaustion in watching the inspiring spectacle; but ere long their high enthusiasm was turned to the deepest discouragement, for, when night fell and after a short march they reached the wells of Alush, it was discovered that the desert tribe which had encamped there yesterday had choked the spring, which at best was but brackish, with stones and rubbish.

"All the water they had carried with them had been used before reaching Dophkah, and the exhausted spring at the mines had not sufficed to fill the skins. Thirst, which at first had only dried their gums, now began to burn their vitals. Their scorched throats could not swallow the solid food of which they had an abundance. On every side there was nothing to be seen but heartbroken looks and pitiable or disgraceful scenes. Men and women storming, cursing, weeping, and groaning, or else sunk in morose despair. Some, whose wailing infants clamored for water, had gathered round the choked well and were fighting for a spot on the ground where they hoped to collect a few drops of the precious fluid in a shard, and the beasts lowed and bleated so miserably that it cut their drivers to the heart like a reproach."

Alush is one of the stations not mentioned in Exodus, although it seems to be implied in Exodus xvii. 1. It is brought into the inspired catalogue given in the thirty-third chapter of Numbers because of the important lessons it teaches. It contains one of the richest "parables" (1 Cor. x. 11) of the whole journey. The word means "leavening," and represents the gradual spread of God's kingdom within us (Matt. xiii. 33). The new leaven enters the heart, and with many secret stirrings and much commotion changes it into its own nature. These were hard experiences at Alush, but they were designed to bring the hearts of the people into full surrender to Jehovah.

The word "leaven" is used seventy-one times in the Old Testament and seventeen times in the New. Sometimes it is the literal mixing of the buoyant principle with the meal that is spoken of, and sometimes it is used figuratively of the spread and rising of either good or evil in the heart. (See Gen. xix. 3; Exod. xii. 15–20; Matt. xvi. 6, 12; Mark viii. 15.)

1. At our Alush station we are to learn that both evil and good work in society like leaven. Some eminent Bible students make leaven always the type of evil; but it seems truer to understand it as representing *growth* by *inward agitation,* and this may apply to both good and evil. At first the good may have little influence and the evil may exert but a moderate power; but friendship helps both along; kindness and sympathy may make of one's fellow a Christian or a man

whose soul is steeped in iniquity; there are a thousand agencies for helping on the leaven of sin and thousands for spreading the influence of truth.

2. As to the growth of sin, study Luke xvii. 26–30 (cf. Gen. vi. 5), xviii. 8, xxi. 34–36; 1 Thessalonians v. 3; 2 Thessalonians ii. 1–12; 1 Timothy iv. 1, 2; 2 Timothy iii. 1–5; Matthew xxiv. compared with Revelation vi.

3. As to the spreading of the kingdom in the heart, study Hebrews ii. 11, x. 9, 14, 29, xiii. 12; 1 Corinthians i. 30; 1 Timothy iv. 4, 5; Ephesians v. 25, 26; 2 Thessalonians ii. 13; 1 Thessalonians iv. 1–4.

4. Alush comes properly after Dophkah, both in the desert wanderings of Israel and in our hearts' experience. For when once we have presented earnest supplication (typified in Dophkah) unto God, the leavening of the holy kingdom within us (figured in Alush) begins to stir and spread. True prayer is the Christian's "vital air," and it is the means and measures of the Christian's progress in sanctification.

How beautifully does our Lord's image of the leaven reveal the nature of sanctification! It is a *gradual* process; it progresses with much *stirring* and *commotion;* but there is no noise or show. The agitation is internal. The heart melts more and more under the droppings of divine dew. More and more does "the goodness of God lead to repentance." Thus progresses that kingdom in the heart which "consisteth not in word, but in power" (1 Cor. iv. 20). Oh, that that purifying, elevating power might be ours more and more! "Sanctify us through Thy truth!"

XI

REPHIDIM

It was only a feverish rest the people had at Alush. There was more watching and murmuring than sleeping. Consequently it was with relief that they heard the sound of the cow-horn which in the early morning, while the stars were still bright in the cloudless sky, gave the signal to press forward again. Let us try to form a mental picture of the day's struggling advance through the mountain defiles—the misery, thirst, uncertainty of it; the bellowing of cattle, the sobs of children, the curses of strong men, the wailing of the women. Moses had gone on ahead; the people knew not where he was. Not until afterward did they know that he was praying most earnestly to Jehovah. Let us go slowly over in mind all the events recorded in the seventeenth and eighteenth chapters of Exodus, for all of these are set down for the Rephidim stage of the people's journey. When Moses comes to catalogue the journeys in the thirty-third chapter of Numbers he simply calls attention to the lack of water at Rephidim (verse 14). This was the most noticeable and painful feature. But all that we find in the graphic chapters of Exodus above referred to occurred in the vicinity.

It is the most brilliant scene we have as yet met in the flight of the Hebrew tribes.

The word "Rephidim" may mean either "the weakening" or "the strengthening of hands." The explanation of this apparent paradox may be drawn from a careful study of the account given in Exodus.

1. In the first place, Israel became weak. They murmured and cried for water, they reviled Moses and blasphemed God (Exod. xvii. 2-4). Here is an example of the unbelief into which God's people too often fall when a little of the temporal good of earth fails them. Here we see also (verse 2) that unbelief is tempting God. Study also Deuteronomy vi. 16 (cf. Exod. xvii. 7); Psalm lxxviii. 18, 41; Matthew iv. 7.

By means of this weakness God brought strength to Israel. He brought them very low and then He helped them. He made them to acknowledge their nothingness, and so they turned to Him for help (verse 5). What a beautiful example does the very word "Rephidim" bring to us, that when we are weak then are we strong! When our knees fail us then are our "hands strengthened" in prayer.

2. God strengthened the hands of Israel also by giving them nourishment. He caused water to flow from Horeb (Exod. xvii. 6). This rock is a type of Christ (1 Cor. x. 4) and of the nourishment God gives us in Him. We may even notice these four particulars in which this rock is a type of Christ: (*a*) Neither of them gave outward evidence of the riches it contained (Isa. liii. 2). (*b*) Both were smitten (Mark xv. 19). (*c*) Both yielded heavenly nourishment (John iv. 13, 14, vii. 37). (*d*) Both yielded a permanent supply

(Matt. xxviii. 19, 20). Oh, let us drink of Christ, that we thirst not again, nor go to the wells of earth to draw!

3. God strengthened the hands of Israel at Rephidim by granting them, in the third place, a victory over Amalek (Exod. xxvii. 8-16). The Amalekites were an old race of Bedouin Arabs occupying the northern portions of the peninsula of Arabia. During the hot, dry months of the year it was their custom to migrate to the valleys and high lands of the mountains near Rephidim. Hence it was that they came in contact with the Israelites at this stage in their progress. The name "Amalek" signifies "hidden locust," and this sheik is a type of those secret and wily temptations which assail the heart in our journey to heaven. A paragraph may be quoted from Ebers to show the style of warfare carried on by the Amalekites:

"At the first onslaught Joshua led forward the men whom he had armed with the large Egyptian shields and lances, and these, fired by their valiant leader, made a good stand, particularly as the narrow defile into the field of battle hindered their wild opponents from taking full advantage of their superior numbers. But when the men on foot presently withdrew, and a troop of warriors on dromedaries rushed down on the Hebrews, many of them were scared at the strange sight of these creatures, known to them only by description. They cast away their shields and fled with loud outcries, and wherever a gap was made the riders drove in their dromedaries and thrust down at the foe with their long, sharp javelins. At this the herdsmen, unused to such an attack, thought only of saving themselves, and many turned to fly, for sudden terror seized them as they saw the flaming eyes and heard the shrill, malignant cry of the enraged Amalekite women, who had rushed into the fight to add fuel to their husbands' courage and terrify the enemy. They held on to the humped brutes by leathern straps hanging down from the saddles, which they clutched in their left hands, and allowed themselves to be dragged whithersoever the riders went. Hatred seemed to have steeled each female heart against fear of death, compassion, and womanly feeling; and the hideous cry of these Negæras broke the spirit of many a brave Hebrew."

4. Amalek cut off the stragglers (Deut. xxv. 17, 18), and sin, in like manner, is most successful in its assaults upon those who are farthest from God and the tabernacle (Mark xiv. 54; cf. 68. If Peter had followed Christ more closely he might not have denied his Lord). God gave victory over Amalek and gives the Christian victory over temptation (1 Cor. x. 13. Note how this tenth chapter of 1 Corinthians follows exactly the occurrences at Rephidim in drawing spiritual lessons). And our victories must be gained by the exercise of these same two agencies: Moses on the mount—*prayer;* and Joshua in the plain—*endeavor.* Prayer and endeavor will enable us to conquer if Jesus (typified in Joshua) be the object of our petition and the motive of our endeavor (Luke i. 69–71).

5. God "strengthens our hands" by these same means—by showing us our weakness, by giving us the water of life, and by granting us spiritual victory. Well may we to-day erect in this, our Rephidim stage of the heavenly journey, an altar such as Moses set up, and

call it with new meaning, "Jehovah-nissi;" for the Lord truly is our banner! (Ps. lx. 4.) This is the first time that we read that "Moses built an altar." It was in part to celebrate the victory that had just been gained and in part to recall to the minds of the Israelites that they were near the spot where God, appearing in the burning bush in Horeb, had said, "Certainly I will be with thee; and this shall be a token unto thee: ... When thou hast brought forth the people out of Egypt, ye shall serve God upon this mountain. ... I AM THAT I AM" (Exod. iii. 12, 14). That promise is now fulfilled.

6. Here at Rephidim occurred the beautiful incident of the visit of Jethro (Exod. xviii.). Moses was now near his old home in Midian. He had married the daughter of Jethro, the priest of Midian, and it must have been a sore trial to him to leave his wife and two sons with her father when he went back to Egypt to deliver his brethren. Jethro, hearing now of his son-in-law's approach, brings the little family to meet him. It is an exquisite bit of Oriental description; read it carefully (verses 5-12). Here, also, we obtain a glimpse into the piety of this Midianite priest, who used the same altar that Moses had just built and conformed to the rules of the burnt-sacrifice, "even to the endearing fellowship expressed by the family gathering to partake of the parts of the sacrifice not consumed upon the altar." Here, also, we see a foretelling—all the more beautiful because unconscious—of the time when Jew and Gentile shall unite together in the faith and worship of "the Lamb that was slain."

XII

SINAI

AFTER the splendid victory over Amalek the people "departed from Rephidim, and pitched in the wilderness of Sinai" (Num. xxxiii. 15). Moses and Joshua began to feel that something more than they possessed was necessary to keep the people obedient. Reverse caused them to murmur, and success threw them into excess. Ebers gives a graphic picture of the approach to the holy mount. It was early morning after the battle, and Joshua had caused the trumpets to be sounded: "He was soon marching at the head of his troops through the narrow gorge, and after they had gone forward for about an hour in silence and in darkness they were refreshed by the cooler air which precedes the day. Dawn began to spread in the east and the sky grew paler, and the glowing splendors of sunrise solemnly and grandly rose above the majestic mass of the holy mountain. It lay spread out before the pilgrims, almost tangibly close and clear, with its brown crags, precipices, and ravines; towering above them rose its seven-peaked crown, round which a pair of eagles were soaring, their broad wings bathed in golden glory in the light of the new-born day.

"And again, as at Alush, a pious thrill brought the marching host to a standstill, while each one, from the first to the last, raised his hands in silent adoration and prayer. Then the warriors went on with hearts uplifted, one gaily calling to another in glad excitement as some pretty little brown birds flew to meet them, twittering loudly, an assurance that fresh water must be near. Hardly half an hour farther on they saw the blue-green foliage of a tamarisk-brake, and above it tall palms, and heard at last the sweetest sounds that ever fall on the listening ear in the desert, the babbling of a running stream. This encouraged them greatly, and the mighty form of the peak of Sinai, its heaven-kissing head veiled in blue mist, filled the souls of these men, dwellers until now in the level meads of Goshen, with devout amazement.

"They now proceeded with caution, for the remnant of the stricken Amalekites might be lurking in ambush. But there was no foe to be seen or heard, and the only traces the Hebrews found of the sons of the desert and their thirst for revenge were their ruined houses, the fine palms felled and prone, and the garden ground destroyed. They were forced to clear the slender trunks out of their path that they might not check the advance of the Hebrew multitude; and when this task was done Joshua went down through a defile leading to the brook in the valley, and up the nearest boulder of the mountain, to look about him far and near for the enemy. The mountain path led over masses of granite veined with green diorite, rising steeply till it ended high above the plain of the oasis at a plateau where, by a clear spring, green shrubs of delicate mountain flowers graced the wilderness. Here he paused to rest, and, looking round, he discerned in the shadow of an overhanging rock a tall figure gazing at the ground.

"It was Moses. The course of his reflections had so completely rapt him from his present surroundings that he did not perceive Joshua's approach, and the warrior reverently kept silence for fear of disturbing the man of God, waiting patiently till he raised his bearded face and greeted him with dignity and kindness. Side by side, they gazed down into the oasis and the desolate, rocky ravines at their feet. Even a tiny strip of the Red Sea which bathes the western foot of the mountains gleamed like an emerald in the distance. And their talk was of the people and of the greatness and power of God, who had brought them so far with such wondrous works; and as they looked to the northward they could see the endless train of the pilgrims, slowly making their way along the devious way of the defile toward the oasis.

"Then did Joshua open his heart to the man of God, and told him all he had thought and wondered during the past sleepless night, finding no answer. The prophet listened to him with composure, and then replied in a deep, hesitating voice and in broken sentences: 'Insubordination in camp—yes; it is ruining the people. But the Lord of might has left it in these hands to dash them to pieces. Woe to those who rebel. That power, as stupendous as this mountain and as immovable as its foundation-rock—they must feel it!' Here the angry speech of Moses ceased. After they had stood for a while looking into the distance, Joshua broke the silence by inquiring, 'And what is that power called?' And the answer came clear and strong from the bearded lips of the man of God: 'The law,' and he pointed with his staff to the top of the peak."

Indeed, it was the law that the people needed. They had been on the march about six weeks, and had taken a journey of one hundred and sixty miles. Abundantly had it been demonstrated that God must give them strong restraints in order to keep them within bounds. Therefore, "in the third month" of their pilgrimage (Exod. xix. 1–3) we find them led to this lonely desert spot, inclosed with high peaks, five thousand feet above the sea. God would have them alone with Himself, away from all that could remind them of their Egyptian life. The pillar of cloud that had gone before them all the way rested now on the top of Sinai. On the third day, in the morning, the Lord came down attended by myriads of angels (Deut. xxxiii. 2; Acts vii. 53; Gal. iii. 19; Heb. ii. 2). Moses goes up to Him, and the magnificent series of events, which can never be exhausted, begins. Study carefully the account in Exodus.

There is a station in every Christian's journey to heaven that corresponds with Sinai. We need to learn the same lessons that were imparted to Israel before the fiery mount. Pi-hahiroth and Elim and Rephidim may be more to our taste; but we cannot get to Canaan without passing by Sinai. We need to pause before the rocky height where God sits in majesty; and, though it take a year (the time consumed by Israel before Sinai) to learn them, we need to learn these three things:

1. *God is a God of justice.*

Israel needed this lesson, and so do we. Before they came to Sinai God excused their murmurings and sins. It was the time of their ignorance, and God "winked" at their disobedience (Acts xvii. 30). But after they had passed Sinai God punished them severely for their defections. This justice of God was shown vividly to the people in the fire which descended upon the mount (Exod. xix. 18); and at our Sinai state we learn, in like manner, that "our God is a consuming fire" (Heb. xii. 29). Of course God's justice has two sides, and if it be severe to punish it is strict to save them who are in Christ.

2. *Sin is a hideous thing.*

Sinai is the place where we learn to understand sin. "By the law is the knowledge of sin" (Rom. iii. 20). The literal meaning of the name "Sinai" is "the ten brambles." It is the same word as "sin," which we have met before, except that the Hebrew letter *jod*, signifying "ten," is added to it. The rabbis used to explain this by showing how the ten commandments are thorns in the natural inclinations of men. Hence it happens that *by the commandment* sin becomes exceeding sinful (Rom. vii. 13). Before Sinai we see that God has the "fire of law" in His right hand (Deut. xxxiii. 2, marg.), and so we are not so apt to judge others (Matt. vii. 1), or to judge according to appearance (John vii. 24), but to *judge ourselves* (1 Cor. xi. 31, 32).

3. *The Christian needs inward purification.*

It was in a bramble-bush in some part of this mountain that God's presence appeared in the form of fire to Moses. This bush, the rabbis thought, was a type of man's soul (Micah vii. 4), and the fire in it typifies God's purifying presence (Isa. xxxi. 9 ; Deut. xxxiii. 16 ; 2 Cor. vi. 16 ; Mark ix. 49). Oh, that we might "be salted," i.e., purified "by fire"; then we would not bow down to the golden calves of earth! (Exod. xxxii. 4 ; 1 John v. 21.)

Ah, the law made nothing perfect. The fires of Sinai could not wholly destroy or wholly restrain sin. The law is only the pedagogue, or servant, to lead the disciple to Christ. By the law we are convicted and aroused to powerful inward sensations of guilt, through the operation of the Holy Spirit. Christ alone can save.

XIII

KIBROTH-HATTAAVAH

BEAUTIFUL and striking is the story locked up in these two unfamiliar words! The mention of them in Numbers xxxiii. 16 does not seem very promising at first, though the margin tells us that the meaning of the name is "the graves of lust." We need to turn back to the tenth and eleventh chapters of Numbers in order to get the story. The station is also mentioned in Deuteronomy ix. 22. Notice that we leave Exodus now, the latter chapters of that book and the whole of Leviticus having to do with the Sinai stage. The Book of Numbers takes up the story of what occurred after the law had been given on the holy mount. It deals with *warfare*, but it is not a record of the devotion of earnest warriors. It gives us rather the sad picture of failure and cowardice. The key-note of Numbers, therefore, is, " Sinners against their own lives."

Let us take up the story (Num. x., xi.). We learn from Deuteronomy i. 6, 7, that when Israel had dwelt almost a year at Sinai, God said, " Ye have dwelt long enough in this mount: turn you, and take your journey." So on the twentieth day of the second month, in the second year, the cloud was taken up as a signal to start

(Num. x. 11). Near the wilderness of Sinai was the wilderness of Paran, and into this the Israelites go. The people march now in regular corps (Num. x. 14-28). Before the start was made Moses makes his touching appeal to Hobab: "Come thou with us, and we will do thee good: . . . thou mayest be to us instead of eyes" (Num. x. 29-31). What a beautiful picture of the good we *get* and the good we *can do* by joining God's people on their march! But Hobab would not go. He preferred the barrenness of the rocks of Midian to the milk and honey of the Promised Land. Alas, how many Hobabs there are in our modern homes and congregations!

For three days the ark of the covenant went before the people, searching for a suitable resting-place for them (Num. x. 33). In the morning Moses broke out in his pæan of praise: "Rise up, Lord, and let Thine enemies be scattered;" and at night Moses softly prayed: "Return, O Lord, unto the ten thousand thousands of Israel" (Num. x. 35, 36, marg.). It was a time of weary searching for a camping-place, but at last they found one—some sheltered spot where grass was abundant and where were wide stretches upon which the manna might fall. It seems that at first this station was called Taberah, "a burning," "because the fire of the Lord burnt among them" (Num. xi. 3).

Then the people began to lust for flesh. Read the whole sad picture in the eleventh chapter of Numbers. Notice the attitude and prayer of Moses. See the choice and enduement of the seventy elders. Observe the parenthetical story of Eldad and Medad, upon whom the Spirit came in an extraordinary manner.

The name "Eldad" means "the love of God," and the name "Medad," "the justice of God." These are the only names given, but beautifully do they show what should be the characteristics of all elders. (See 2 Sam. xxiii. 3, 4.) After this we have the story of the giving of the quails, the gathering of them by the people, the anger of the Lord, the great plague, and the changing of the name of the station to Kibroth-hattaavah, "because there they buried the people that lusted" (Num. xi. 30–34).

Standing in the place where we find it, the eleventh chapter of Numbers is of thrilling interest. Israel had just received the law, and the law said, "Thou shalt not lust" (Rom. vii. 7). Yet at the first station after Sinai we find them giving way to concupiscence. The interest of this station also grows out of the fact that Israel might soon have entered into the promised possessions if it had not been for their unbelief and lust. Ah, how many blessings do we just miss because of our sin! (Matt. xiii. 58.)

At this station we learn:

1. *That there is contagion in sin.*

There had come a "mixed multitude" out of Egypt with Israel, and from this came the temptation to sin (Num. xi. 4). Evil is contagious. Even in the regenerate heart there are two natures warring against each other (Rom. vii. 19–25). The old Adam is never wholly eradicated until you cross the Jordan. And after the "mixed multitude" got well to murmuring, the contagion spread to all Israel.

2. *That there is worldliness in sin.*

The poor wife of Lot looks back lovingly to the delights of Sodom. The unbelieving Israelites desire the onions and leeks and the garlic of Egypt. When sin is thoroughly analyzed there is always an element of worldliness in it. The defaulter thinks he will get worldly happiness out of his unlawful gains, and the drunkard imagines the hallucinations of intoxication to be the delights of life. Then see how Israel was punished for murmuring, now that Sinai is passed (Num. xi. 33). The law is given, and offenses against the law cannot be forgotten, as they were before Sinai (1 Cor. x. 6).

3. *That there is discontent in sin.*

Israel had manna, but wanted flesh. How wonderful is God's patience in providing them with quails! While we admire this, let us not fail to learn the lesson in 1 Timothy vi. 6–12, a passage which certainly is a striking paraphrase of Israel's experience at Kibrothhattaavah.

XIV

HAZEROTH

WE may fairly judge from the narrative that the children of Israel tarried for some time at Hazeroth, which was their next station in their journey Canaanward. The last verse of the eleventh chapter of Numbers tells us that they "abode" at Hazeroth; in the seventeenth verse of the thirty-third chapter of Numbers it is implied that they established one of their fixed and permanent camps there. Possibly grass and water were plentiful at this point, and the people tarried to enjoy one of those periods of rest and refreshment which God, in His mercy, afforded them even in the desert. A glance at the map will show that it is not a long journey from the last stopping-place to Hazeroth. It was downhill from the high valleys before Mount Sinai, and it was considerably nearer the Gulf of Ælana, whose waters are still bordered with luxuriant foliage. The mountains to the westward would catch the clouds arising from the gulf, and frequent, if not copious, rainfalls would cause the grass to grow. Every natural feature of the valley running down to the gulf, broadening as it runs, conforms to the hints we have in the passage above referred to. The prevailing winds, also, are from the northeast, blowing from the wide reaches of the land of Moab, and, as there are no mountains to the eastward of the gulf, these winds would bear the moisture straight into the valley of Hazeroth to be condensed into rain against the western hills. It was an oasis in their hard journey. Amalek had been discomfited, and from the other desert tribes they were guarded on the one side by the mountains and on the other by the gulf. With the Midianites, through whose country they were now marching, they were at peace because of the marriage of Moses to the daughter of the priest of Midian, the wise and kindly Jethro.

Ah, but this beautiful spot witnessed sad events! Encouraged to false pride by the security and plenty, the people began to think they could do without God. Even "Miriam and Aaron spake against Moses" (Num. xii. 1), and the righteous judgment of God was again called forth. Read the twelfth chapter of Numbers very carefully to see how ease and plenty are apt to lead us into sin. "Hazeroth" means literally "a division" so great as to cause *trembling;* and to this day we cannot read the account of what transpired there without being filled with fear because of the prevalence of sin in the world and its sure punishment.

Our lesson to-day is, therefore, for the favored, the rich, the distinguished—those who are at ease, whether in the world or in Zion. The thrilling commentary on our lesson is found in the words of Christ: "How hardly shall they that have riches enter into the kingdom of God!" (Mark x. 23.)

At this station we learn:

1. *How much evil the tongue can do.*

The whole matter was a family dispute, and every one knows how bitter such a thing usually becomes. Miriam and Aaron began to whisper tales derogatory to the wife of Moses (Num. xii. 1, 2). How many of the defections of the Israelites grew out of an unwise use of the tongue! Almost always one can detect in the narrative the distant murmuring of discontented voices before there is audible and open outbreak. One of the most pithy and striking passages in the whole Bible is that in which St. James describes the evil the tongue may cause (James iii. 1–13). And at Hazeroth we are also shown that envy is the real gall in most of the bitterness of the tongue (Num. xii. 2; cf. James iii. 14–18). All the possessions of Haman, all the faithful love of Zeresh, all the kindliness of his friends, the glory of his riches, the multitude of his children, the promotion of the king, and the invitations of the queen—all were rendered worthless by envy "so long as he saw Mordecai the Jew sitting at the king's gate" (Esth. v. 10–13).

2. *How wrong it is to disregard the teachings of the Bible.*

God came down and "spake suddenly" to the talkers of malice (Num. xii. 4). He tells them with what sacredness His prophets are invested, and He talks plainly of the respect all men owe to them. Notice that it is in this connection that the statement is made that Moses was "very meek, above all the men which were on the face of the earth." Observe also the distinction God puts between Moses, with whom "He spake mouth to mouth," and an ordinary prophet, to whom truth was revealed "in dark speeches." Oh, there is a blessed nearness to God through the Spirit into which we may all come by meekness of disposition and absolute surrender to the truth! God speaks to us "face to face" in the Bible, and we should be afraid to speak against the Word (Num. xii. 8). How sad it is to see Christians questioning the Scriptures, or making their holy teachings a theme of ridicule or jest. We would do well to study such passages as the following, and to notice the sacredness of the Bible implied in them: Psalm cxix. 18, 81, 82; Revelation i. 3, xxii. 19.

3. *How much evil one Christian may do.*

The whole company had to wait until Miriam was restored from her leprosy (Num. xii. 15); and may not a whole church be compelled to wait upon one thoughtless or sinful Christian? Oh, it is a fearful thing to be the Achan of a camp! When the question arises as to who is to betray the Lord by coldness or sinfulness, we ought each to take up the sorrowful question of the disciples: "Lord, is it I?" Timely self-examination may help us to avoid a sin which much and bitter repentance will not set right again. Notice that "doing foolishly" (verse 11) is often quite as bad as that which we call flagrant sinning. See how Moses prays, and yet how God uses both divine wisdom and infinite tenderness in answering. The relations between these three human beings, members of one household, so clearly brought out in this chapter and so wisely arranged by the tender Father over all, may well be a picture for careful study in modern homes.

XV

RITHMAH

WE come now to a number of stations which are catalogued in the thirty-third chapter of Numbers, but are not mentioned elsewhere in the Bible. Neither the Sinaitic Survey Party nor any individual traveler has been able to identify them. Ezion-gaber (Num. xxxiii. 35) has been located, as may be seen by a glance at the map of the Sinaitic peninsula; but there are seventeen stations recorded between Hazeroth and Ezion-gaber of which we know nothing. The probabilities are that these were all in the wilderness of Paran, into which the Israelites entered as soon as Miriam had recovered of her leprosy (Num. xii. 16).

Rithmah may have been the place from which the spies were sent out to "search the land of Canaan" (Num. xiii. 2). Then during the forty days occupied by the search the Israelites may have journeyed to Rimmon-parez and some other stations. It is said in Numbers xiii. 26 that the spies brought back their report to "Kadesh"; but this could hardly be the place called Kadesh-barnea. It means probably the whole district of Paran, and in this Rithmah was situated.

At all events, it will be best for us to consider here

the whole story of the spies and their report. There were twelve of them altogether. How they were chosen, who they were, what they saw, and what report they made we have graphically described in the thirteenth and fourteenth chapters of Numbers. Ten of them discouraged the people with a dismal report of the giants of Anak and the warriors among the tribes of Canaan. Only two, Caleb and Joshua, encouraged the Israelites to advance. With startling effect is the difference between the fearful and trustful brought out in these counter-reports. The unbelieving ten said, " The people be strong that dwell in the land, and the cities are walled, and very great: and moreover we saw the children of Anak there." We can almost hear them catch their breath with fright as they recount these particulars. And then, with disjointed haste, they go on to say, " The Amalekites dwell in the land of the south: and the Hittites, and the Jebusites, and the Amorites, dwell in the mountains: and the Canaanites dwell by the sea, and by the coast of Jordan." These were hard and unfamiliar names to the people, and no wonder that the timid report filled them with affright. On the other hand, hear the strong words of the noble two: " Let us go up at once, and possess it; for we are well able to overcome it; . . . neither fear ye the people of the land; for they are bread for us: their defense is departed from them, and the Lord is with us." Here we have the exact difference between the useless and the useful men of to-day—the one being timid and unbelieving and the other faithful and strong.

The meaning of the word " Rithmah " is " the place of bonds," and in view of the discussion that took place there it is very expressive; for there the people fell into the bondage of unbelief. In this light how full of meaning is the apostle's injunction in Galatians v. 1! Some Hebrew scholars say that "Rithmah" means "the place of junipers," because here the mischievous tongues of the ten spies brought the evil report, and were hence like the "coals of juniper," which burn extremely (Ps. cxx. 4).

The lessons for us at this station are:

1. *The fear of men brings bondage.*

The Israelites failed because they had regard for the giants of Anak. Many a man fails because he does not realize that God is greater than man. Pilate feared men. They said to him, "You are not Cæsar's friend." That decided him to crucify the Lord of the whole earth. Thus he came into the bondage of sin.

2. *Faith in God brings success.*

Let us who have read of Israel's failure avoid the cause of it. Let us trust in God, and fear not. Then we may go forward to a grand success.

3. *We have two special encouragers.*

The Israelites had two encouragers, Joshua and Caleb. Now Joshua is the same name as Jesus, and the literal meaning of the name "Caleb" is "a good heart." May we not say, therefore, that the Christian has two encouragers to advance, *Jesus* (Matt. x. 26, 28; Luke viii. 50, xii. 32; Acts xxvii. 24; Rev. i. 17) and *a good heart* (2 Cor. vii. 1; Tit. ii. 13, 14)?

With Jesus and a good heart the conquest of our spiritual possessions becomes an easy matter. How sweetly does the Master point out to us the secret of our strength: "He that abideth in Me, and I in him, the same bringeth forth much fruit; for without Me ye can do nothing"! (John xv. 5.)

4. *Sin in general and in particular brings bondage.*

The whole life of Israel in Egypt illustrates this. Eleven times Moses speaks of Egypt as "the house of bondage." The thought is carried bodily into the New Testament. He who serves sin becomes the slave of sin, whether it be sin in general or some particular sin. (See John viii. 34; Rom. vi. 16; Tit. iii. 3: "Serving divers lusts and pleasures"—the slave and drudge of many masters; 2 Pet. ii. 19: "The servants of corruption.")

5. *Man sells himself into bondage.*

The saddest thing of all is that a man may sell himself into slavery to sin; indeed, he must do this if he come into bondage at all, for no one can impose captivity upon him but himself. Ahab did this. (See 1 Kings xxi. 20.) Israel did this. (See 2 Kings xvii. 17; Isa. l. 1. See also Rom. vii. 23.)

In times past many nations have been disgraced by their customs of slavery; and, indeed, in our own times it is impossible quite to stamp out the dreadful slave-trade on the coasts of Africa. Kings and counselors, empires and republics, have countenanced the bondage of lower races of men and innocent women and children. It is a distressing picture. But how much more distressing when men and women deliberately sell themselves into the power of Satan, the relentless overseer and taskmaster!

Flee, then, dear soul, to Jesus, who will make you free indeed! (John viii. 36.) The prophecy concerning Him was that He should be anointed to give liberty to the captives (Isa. lxi. 1). And, more than this, —as it was the custom in the old days to burn out the eyes of slaves and captives,—it is even said that Jesus will restore sight to such as have been blinded thus by sin. (See Luke iv. 18.) Glorious thought! Oh, that we may, through Christ and the power of the Spirit, "awake ourselves out of the snare of the devil, having been taken alive by him at his will"! (2 Tim. ii. 26, marg.)

XVI

RIMMON-PAREZ

This is one of the most interesting stations in all the course of Israel to the Promised Land. It is another of the unmarked stations in the province of Kadesh. It seems probable that while they were encamped here God solemnly declared that, because of their unbelief, they should all perish in the wilderness, with the exception of Joshua and Caleb. They had believed the report of the timid spies, and now, in spite of the earnest prayer of Moses, their carcasses should all be "wasted in the wilderness." All this is described with wonderful vividness in Numbers xiv. and Deuteronomy i. 41-46. Now what would we expect to be the effect of this declaration upon the Israelites? Surely they will repent of their sins and be plunged into the most sincere humiliation; they will bewail their unbelief and cry unto God for help. But nothing of this kind occurs. On the contrary, the people became exceedingly presumptuous, and formed the resolution to go out in their own strength against the Amorites. How ingular is their conduct! At Rithmah we find them murmuring because God was proposing to lead them up against the Canaanites. They actually incurred the divine wrath by their fear when God was ready to support them. Here we find them ready to undertake in their own strength a perilous and presumptuous campaign. What a faithful picture is this of the human heart! Man will undertake to do anything, even to the saving of his soul, in his own name; but he will fear to enter upon a safe and joyous religious life, with God for his guide and strength.

The Israelites went out in their own strength against the Amorites and the Amalekites, and, rushing up the hill upon which their enemies were encamped, they began the attack with inconsiderate haste. God was not with them, and of course they were overcome. They were driven back as far as Hormah, which signifies "destruction," and then they returned disconsolately to their camp at Rimmon-parez. It was from this circumstance that this camp received its name. "Rimmon-parez" means literally "tribulation because of elevation." They were afflicted and smitten because of the lifting up of their pride and self-confidence. "Pride goeth before destruction, and a haughty spirit before a fall" (Prov. xvi. 18). Notice the fearful indictment brought by the author of Proverbs against pride (viii. 13, xi. 2, xiii. 10, xiv. 3, xxi. 24, xxix. 23).

The destruction which is indicated in the word "Parez" is often represented in Scripture under the figure of a "breach" made in the walls of a city in the day of battle, or in the bank of a river by the fierce current. Two places we know of were named from circumstances which remind us of the desert station we are now considering. In 1 Chronicles xiii. 10, 11, we read that Uzza "put his hand to the ark," and God smote him, "wherefore that place is called Perez-uzza to this day." The margin tells us that this name means "the breach" or destruction of Uzza, and it is the same Hebrew word that we have in our study to-day. The second example we find in 1 Chronicles xiv. 11, where a place called Baal-perazim is mentioned, so named because David said, "God hath broken in upon mine enemies by mine hand like the breaking forth of waters." The margin translates this for us, "a place of breaches." The Hebrew word also occurs in Genesis xxxviii. 29; Judges xxi. 15; 2 Samuel v. 20; 1 Kings xi. 27; Nehemiah vi. 1; Job xvi. 14; Isaiah xxx. 13; Amos iv. 3; and several other passages of the Old Testament.

At this station we may learn the following lessons:

1. *How sudden the change from discouragement to presumption.*

The Christian must be conscious frequently of passing from Rithmah to Rimmon-parez—from discouragement to undue self-reliance. Human nature swings in a pendulum course, and we must expect as extreme changes as this station of Israel witnessed. The picture in the fourteenth chapter of Numbers is true to life. Moses told the Lord's sayings to the people (verse 39). Clearly was it pointed out that for forty years they should wander about the desert until all were dead, save only the two faithful spies, Caleb and Joshua, and the feeble little children (verse 31). Notice how God includes the children, for the very reason that the unbelieving Israelites had made them an excuse for murmuring. "Our children will perish before the great giants of the land," the people had cried.

God says, "I will prove My power to you by bringing your children to Canaan,—these very little ones you seem to be so timid of,—while you yourselves shall die in the wilderness." Then the people "mourned greatly" (verse 39). And on the very top of this mourning they get up and defy Moses and the Lord! "They presumed to go up unto the hilltop" to fight (verse 44). It seems an incredible mutation of character, and yet it is perfectly true to human nature.

Two New Testament churches are distinguished for their pride and presumption—Laodicea (Rev. iii. 17) and Corinth. It is worth remembering that the word "boasting" and its derivatives occur twenty-nine times in 2 Corinthians, and only twenty-six times in all the rest of St. Paul's epistles. See, also, how two other apostles speak of the matter—St. James (iv. 6) and St. Peter (1 Pet. v. 6). "Keep back Thy servant also from presumptuous sins" (Ps. xix. 13) is a prayer that will never be outworn.

2. *It is dangerous fighting against sin without God's aid.*

Only dismal defeat can be expected. The literal meaning of the word "Amalekites" is "hidden locusts," and of "Canaanite" is "a trading or worldly spirit." In like manner, secret sins and worldliness are the principal things that the Christian needs to combat. And as Israel could by no means prevail against these without God's aid, no more can we conquer in life's temptations without divine assistance. See what a perfect summation of a Rimmon-parez experience in the inner life we have in 1 Peter v. 5: "God resisteth the proud [setteth Himself in battle array against this type of character], and giveth grace to the humble." And this grace brings with it victory. Let us not forget the wise direction of the apostle who had tried fighting alone, and had also tested the armor of God (Eph. vi. 13).

3. *We must attempt nothing without Moses and the ark—the law and the gospel.*

We are to take a remembrance of the terrors of the law and the restraints of the gospel with us into all our pleasures and all our dangers. We must put on the Lord Jesus, our armor of light, and take Moses and the ark with us in all our conflicts, and then we shall conquer. In this connection study Exodus xxxiii. 15; 2 Corinthians xii. 10; Philippians iv. 13.

The ancient Egyptians carried the mummies of their dead ancestors to their feasts, in order that they might remember death in the midst of joys and rejoicings. So should we carry with us at all times a remembrance of the dispensation of Moses. Yet we should not be saddened by it. Christ hath fulfilled the law for us. In Him we have perfect and constant victory. The law should ever be present in our consciousness, not as a threatening taskmaster, but as a tender pedagogue " to lead us to Christ."

XVII

LIBNAH

Soon after leaving Rimmon-parez Israel came to Libnah. A casual reading of the Bible might not give us any idea of the spiritual significance of this short journey. When we give attention to the narrative, however, and take into account the meaning of these stations, we see how all these things were written for our admonition. "Libnah" means literally "whiteness" or "frankincense," and the root from which the word comes is often used in the Bible for "purity" and "prayer." Whiteness is the type of purity, as frankincense is of prayer. Remembering, then, that Rimmon-parez, the last station at which Israel stopped, means "tribulation," we see the spiritual meaning of the narrative. For surely the sorrows of tribulation lead the Christian on to purity of heart, and induce a frame of mind of which prayer is the only satisfactory and satisfying expression.

To justify this interpretation, as well as to encourage our hearts, let us take a few passages of the Bible:

1. *In regard to whiteness, or purity.*

There are many texts that might be quoted in which the root from which the word "Libnah" comes is used to express that moral whiteness, or purity, for which the true child of God longs. As examples, look at

Ecclesiastes ix. 8 : " Let thy garments be always white; and let thy head lack no ointment;" Psalm li. 7 : " Wash me, and I shall be whiter than snow;" Isaiah i. 18: "Though your sins be as scarlet, they shall be as white as snow;" Daniel xi. 35 : " Some of them of understanding shall fall, to try them, and to purge, and to make them white;" and Daniel xii. 10: "Many shall be purified, and made white, and tried." How rich and beautiful are these passages, as showing how the real idea of Libnah is that station in our journey heavenward when past tribulations lead us to desire purity of soul! Many other parts of God's Word might be appealed to to afford us the same lessons. When Paul was in danger of being lifted up with pride, as Israel was at Rimmon-parez, God gave him "a thorn in the flesh, the messenger of Satan to buffet" him (2 Cor. xii. 7–10). So he became ready to confess (Heb. xii. 10) that God's "chastisements are for our profit, that we may be partakers of His holiness."

Whiteness of garment is really an orientalism when used to typify the purity of character coming from affliction, but it is one that every one can understand. A child catches the meaning of Revelation vii. 13–15 : " What are these which are arrayed in white robes? . . . These are they which came out of great tribulation, and have washed their robes, and made them white in the blood of the Lamb. Therefore are they before the throne." Distinctly is it said in Revelation xix. 8 : " The fine linen is the righteousness ["the righteous acts," R. V.] of the saints." And then let us remember the blessed promise of the Master : " They shall walk with Me in white " (Rev. iii. 4). In oriental lands you may still see a host surrounded by his guests, all clothed in white garments, walking together through the banqueting-halls, or along the avenues under the trees out in the park. So Christ promises to be our Host; nay, more blessedly still, our Bridegroom! He will lead us and converse with us, and everything in the mansions of eternity belonging to Him shall be freely placed at our disposal.

2. *In regard to frankincense, or prayer.*

Tribulation also drives us to our knees. It may be interesting and instructive to study the following passages, in all of which the Hebrew root from which " Libnah " comes is used in the sense of frankincense and prayer: Exodus xxx. 30, 34, 35 : Aaron was to be anointed with frankincense in order that he might be an accepted intercessor for the people; Leviticus ii. 1 ; Isaiah xliii. 23, lx. 6. Frankincense was one of the main ingredients of the incense offered upon the altar, and hence it is constantly used as a type of prayer. (See Ps. cxli. 2 ; Rev. v. 8.) And it is interesting to notice that, as the incense was to be offered daily upon the golden altar (Exod. xxx. 7), so is prayer to be repeated daily, nay, hourly, and in all parts of the world (1 Tim. ii. 8).

There is a beautiful verse in Isaiah (xxvi. 16) which exactly expresses the Christian's thoughts and desires when at Libnah on his way to heaven: " Lord, in trouble have they visited Thee, they poured out a prayer when Thy chastening was upon them." And two verses in the Song of Solomon may be studied with profit (iii. 6, iv. 6) : " Who is this that cometh out of the wilderness like pillars of smoke, perfumed with myrrh and frankincense, with all powders of the merchant?" "Until the day break, and the shadows flee away, I will get me to the mountain of myrrh, and to the hill of frankincense." In both of these verses we are to remember that myrrh is a type of bruising or tribulation and that frankincense is ever a type of prayer, and then the meaning is plain. Here in sublime figure we have the word "Libnah" used to show how the truly devout soul flies to prayer when tribulation has come upon it.

There is no frankincense sweeter to the parent than the pleading breath of his loving child. The child is in trouble, is ill, or feels lonely or disappointed. Then it clambers up into the parent's lap and breathes its wish against the parent's cheek. Is there any sweeter odor than that? Poets talk of the "kine's breath" that has been fed upon pure grass and lovely flowers; but the father or mother who has established sympathetic relations with the child knows something more mellow and softly odorous than the kine's breath.

Now God uses the sweetness of a child's soft breath to typify that loving prayer in which He delights. Turn to Isaiah xxvi. 16: "Lord, in trouble have they visited Thee, they poured out a prayer [a whisper or "secret speech," as in marg.] when Thy chastening was upon them." The figure here is precisely that I have suggested—a troubled or lonely child clambering up into the father's lap to whisper out its grief, with its kisses upon the father's cheek. Turn also to Lamentations iii. 56: "Thou hast heard my voice: hide not Thine ear at my *breathing*, at my cry." Oh, God will never hide His ear to such frankincense as that!

XVIII

RISSAH

It must have been dismal business, wandering around in the wilderness of Paran, now that the Israelites knew that all the adults, with two exceptions, were to die without entering into the Promised Land. When there is no prospect of reaching anything except a grave before one, life is by no means rosy. And yet a great many people nowadays seem to be living on no higher plane than this. To get enough manna for the day and to be comfortably clothed against the storms seem to fill up the cup of their ambition. In this life only they have hope, and really they "are of all men most miserable." No citizenship in heaven; no sweet homesickness for the "land of far distances" (Isa. xxxiii. 17, marg.); no aspirations for release from the seen and temporal; no "blessed hope," looking for the coming of the Lord! The gloomy drifting about in the Kadesh regions of the wilderness of Paran is a sad type of that merely worldly life which terminates in the falling of the carcasses into the sand. Ah, but the soul! Yes, that shall live; but the worldly ones give no thought to that.

Notice, however, that God was merciful even when

His judgments were most literally being carried out. We may safely and surely judge from the desert stations mentioned about this time that God began to deal in a very special manner with the inner life of the Israelites. As the outward things became hopeless, the inner hopefulness began to dawn and continued to increase. As the people could not come into the earthly Canaan, God graciously began to prepare them for entering in to the spiritual Canaan at death. Even in Paran He gave them many comforting glimpses of truth and many sweet evidences of His love. As their outward man perished, their inward man was renewed day by day (2 Cor. iv. 16). One pleasing example of this dealing we have before us in this station.

Removing from Libnah, the Israelites came to Rissah (Num. xxxiii. 21), and this is one of the most important and significant journeys of the whole desert course. For "Rissah" means literally "the dropping of dew." The word is constantly used in the Bible to denote refreshment through the descent of God's grace. And remembering that "Libnah" signified "purity" and "prayer," we see the meaning of this journey. It shows how close spiritual refreshment is to a thorough purification of the heart through prayer. Let the faithful Christian in the desert of this world lift up his heart in true devotion, and the dews of God's grace will immediately descend upon it.

1. To show the correctness of this interpretation, turn to the following passages, in all of which the Hebrew root from which "Rissah" comes is used: Song of Solomon v. 2: "The drops of the night;" Amos vi.

11, marg.: this passage gives us a grand scene; under God's curse the stones are represented as dropping out of the wall like drops of heavy dew; Ezekiel xlvi. 14: the word "temper" here is literally "moisten." The oil is a type of spiritual blessings descending upon the heart when the head is anointed. (See also Exod. xxix. 7; cf. verse 21; Ps. cxxxiii. 2, 3; 1 John ii. 20.)

2. How many beautiful passages there are in the Bible promising spiritual refreshment! It comes upon the heart as quietly as the dew upon the flower. It brings a divine and lasting benefit. See how these thoughts are brought out in the following passages: Psalm lxxii. 6: "Like rain upon the mown grass;" Deuteronomy xxxii. 2, 3: "My speech shall distil as the dew;" Hosea xiv. 5: "I will be as the dew unto Israel;" Deuteronomy xxxiii. 13, 28: "Blessed be the Lord . . . for the dew. . . . His heavens shall drop down dew;" Job xxix. 19: "The dew lay all night upon my branch;" Isaiah xxvi. 19: "Thy dew is as the dew of herbs."

Oh, it is worth something to have the refreshment of God's dews descending upon the tired, suffering soul!

3. But there is a more specific thought still in this theme. How many of God's saints have found that a blessed Rissah is just beyond a painful Libnah! After the temptations comes the ministering of the angels (Matt. iv. 11). After the prayer comes the sense of peace. Before the supplication the soul may be as barren as the land of Palestine before Elias prayed; but the heavens are sure to open and the fruit is certain to appear (James v. 17, 18). Even our Lord felt the need of prayer and experienced the blessedness

of the answer. In connection with fifteen important events in the life of Christ we find Him praying: at His baptism (Luke iii. 21, 22); after He had healed the sick (Mark i. 35); when His fame spread and the multitudes came to hear (Luke v. 16); when His enemies sought to destroy Him, and before appointing His disciples (Luke vi. 2–12); when He fed the five thousand (Mark viii. 6); when He told the disciples He must be rejected and slain (Luke ix. 18); when He was transfigured (Luke ix. 28); at the grave of Lazarus (John xi. 41); when He taught the disciples how to pray (Luke xi. 1); when His soul was troubled (John xii. 27); when about to leave His disciples in a world of tribulation (John xvii.); in the garden of Gethsemane (Matt. xxvi. 36); at the institution of the Last Supper (Mark xiv. 21–23); for His murderers (Luke xxiii. 34); and when He resigned His breath to the Father (Luke xxiii. 46). The apostles had the same experiences (Acts iv. 31). Oh, if we are to have our churches and our hearts shaken with the mighty Spirit, it must be through prayer!

There is a beautiful verse in John (xvi. 24) where our Saviour brings out the precise change between Libnah and Rissah: "Hitherto have ye asked nothing in My name: *ask*, and ye shall receive, that your *joy* may be full." The longing of the plant is answered by the descending dew filling the chalice of the lily with sparkling moisture. The prayer of the weary heart is answered by the descending joy that fills to overflowing. When we have this joy we cannot but be of service.

What a tender and loving attitude does God assume

at Rissah, where the hearts of the Israelites were particularly dry and desert-like! At the moment of their deepest discouragement He causes the heavy dews of His grace to distil and drop into their souls. Their extremity becomes God's opportunity. He would woo them away from their bitterness and rebellion to perfect trust and peace. And God acts upon the same principle nowadays. He is the same God still. Oh, let us open our deepest hearts to the drops of His comforting dews! Dear Lord, moisten my dry and parched nature in every part! Make it sweet and bright and cool. Lead me, just now, to Rissah!

XIX

KEHELATHAH

"And they journeyed from Rissah, and pitched in Kehelathah" (Num. xxxiii. 22). It is a simple record of God's Word, bearing upon the face of it nothing to indicate the deep spiritual lessons contained in the statement. There is much for us, however, to learn from this record. The divine refreshment and sweet communion with God that the people of Israel enjoyed at Rissah led them on to a desire to "assemble themselves" frequently and earnestly for worship. For "Kehelathah" means, according to its best derivation from the Hebrew root, an "earnest and devout assemblage for worship." The people, having once tasted of the goodness of God, craved communion with Him. They found that it is a good thing to be in the presence of the Father of grace and blessing, and came immediately to desire a frequent enjoyment of the privilege. Oh, it is a short journey from Rissah to Kehelathah! When once the godly soul has fed upon righteousness it learns to hunger and thirst for it. As we remember this we see the meaning of Romans xv. 4. The detailed description of the experiences of Israel in the desert is designed for our instruction, "that we through patience and comfort of the Scriptures might have the hope."

There are several passages in the Bible in which the Hebrew root from which "Kehelathah" comes is used in the sense given in the interpretation above. For example, in Leviticus iv. 21 it is translated "congregation"; in Joshua xviii. 1 the children of Israel are said to "assemble together" at Shiloh to set up the tabernacle. In the Twenty-second Psalm it is said (verse 22): "In the midst of the congregation will I praise Thee," and (verse 25) "My praise shall be of Thee in the great congregation." In Psalm xl. 9 it is also used: "I have preached righteousness in the great congregation;" and it is translated in the following verse with the same word. In Psalm cxlix. 1 we find the same translation. These are specimen passages, showing the correctness of the interpretation of the meaning of "Kehelathah."

But the form of the word which we have in "Kehelathah" has what is known as a "double augmentation." Hebrew scholars will detect this at once. The rule of the Hebrew augmentation is, "The increasing of the word is a sign of the signification increased." So that the name of this station imports the "frequent and earnest assembling" of the people to wait upon God. It was not a mere formal gathering. They assembled not for a perfunctory service. The droppings of the dews of grace upon their hearts had produced a softening and sanctifying effect. What a wonderful picture that churchly gathering must have made! Picture the scene: the scantily clad hills of Paran all around, the rude tents of the wandering people in the near background, and here in the center, clustered around the tabernacle, the devoutly worshiping assembly. It reminds one of the modern gathering of the Northwestern Indians on the plains of Dakota to hear the gospel or to engage in religious discussions. There are the same nomadic peoples, the same rude surroundings, the same bare hills and plains, the same earnest and devout hearts.

Now look at the following passages, showing the increase of faith and joy that every devout Christian attains by attending the worship of the church: Isaiah xlv. 19: "I said not unto the seed of Jacob, Seek ye Me in vain." This verse, and, indeed, the whole passage from which it is taken, refer directly to the experiences of the children of Israel that we have been studying. Matthew xviii. 20: "Where two or three are gathered." This is Christ's own estimate of the value of religious assemblages, and His own promise of blessing. Look also at Hebrews iii. 13, x. 24, 25.

A very profitable study of the eighth chapter of Nehemiah may also be made, where several excellencies of the model church are shown. There are twelve of these, and without them there can neither be a revival nor efficient stated work. A revival really applies to the church-members; the results of a revival may be larger congregations and the conversion of sinners. You cannot *get up* a revival, but you can get one *down* by prayer and holy living (Ps. lxxxv. 6; Hab. iii. 2). The twelve things about the model or revived church, as shown in Nehemiah viii., are:

1. *Unanimity* (verse 1). This is very necessary.

Even the children came to this divine worship (verse 2). (See also Jer. l. 4, 5; Acts ii. 1.)

2. *Interest in God's Word* (verse 3). Without this there can be no revival or usefulness. See a good reputation to have, in Daniel vi. 5. (See also John v. 39.)

3. *Support of the minister's hands* (verse 4). A great many churches are ruined by the senseless criticism indulged in by the people and directed against the pastors. (Refer again to Exod. xvii. 8–12.)

4. *Reverence* (verse 5). This seems to be a lost art in many modern churches. The old people sleep and the young people giggle. It was not so at Kehelathah or in Nehemiah's revival. (See also Heb. xii. 28.)

5. *Prayer and humiliation* (verse 6). There can be no model church without these. (See Isa. lxii. 6, marg.; Zech. iv. 6, 7; Isa. xxxii. 15–17.)

6. *Lay activity* (verse 7). Whatever we may think of lay preaching, there is certain lay activity which no prosperous church can get along without. (See Matt. iii. 11, xiii. 58.)

7. *Faithful preaching of the Word* (verse 8). This is the divinely appointed means for the winning of men to the truth. (See 1 Tim. iv. 15, 16.)

8. *Conviction of sin as a result* (verse 9). This comes about when the truth of the Word is applied to the heart and conscience by the Holy Spirit. (See Matt. xxiii. 29.)

9. *Christian liberality* (verse 10). This is always an accompaniment of the revival. It may go before or it may follow after (Mal. iii. 10; Acts iv. 37, cf. v. 14).

10. *Joy in the truth* (verse 12). This is another result of the revival in a church, and is a constant bless-

ing in the model church. (See Isa. xxv. 6; Ps. li. 12, 13, c. 2.)

11. *Dedication of self* (verse 14). Here we come again to the life of separation, the Succoth experience, which we considered when we were at that station. (Refer again to Exod. viii. 22, 23.)

12. *Transmission of the tidings* (verse 15). When the church is fully aroused this always occurs, and what we know as home missions and foreign missions result. Some one has said that the whole of Christianity lies in these four words: admit, submit, commit, transmit. And, indeed, to admit the truth, submit to the truth, commit one's self entirely to the truth, and then transmit the truth, would be ideal Christian character and life. May the Holy Spirit bring us as individuals, and the churches with which we are connected, to this standard! (See Hos. vi. 1–3; Rev. xxii. 14, 17; Zech. viii. 21.)

There is real danger in this age of the world that the essential quietness and joy of *worship* shall disappear from the sanctuary. The eloquence of the preacher and the artistic elegance of the choir are made too prominent. Worship means literally "worthship." It is the ascribing of worth unto God. Its value resides, therefore, in personal approach to God, personal quietness and trust in Him, personal praise and thought of Him. This seems to have been the frame of mind the people were in when stopping at Kehelathah and when worshiping under the direction of Nehemiah. May God by His Spirit enable us all, and all His church, to realize this quiet joy in worship!

XX

SHAPHER

AFTER the experiences at Kehelathah the Israelites took their journey to Mount Shapher and pitched there (Num. xxxiii. 23). At the former station they had engaged in worship of God, and they enjoyed at Shapher the results of true worship; for "Shapher" means "beauty" or "comeliness." The soul of the earnest and devout Christian becomes beautified under the light of the throne. There is a comeliness of heart and life that sincere worship alone can give. How precious, then, should be our Sabbaths, and especially the hours that are spent in the sanctuary! "Put ye on the Lord Jesus Christ" refers not only to protection, but to the beauty which such a garment imparts to the wearer.

1. *The general teaching of this station.*

In order to grasp the force of the name given to this station by the Israelites in their gladsome fervor let us look at the following passages, in all of which is found the Hebrew root from which "Shapher" comes: Genesis xlix. 21: "Naphtali is a hind let loose: he giveth *goodly* words." In the delight of a worshipful spirit Naphtali dwells at Shapher and speaks goodly or beautiful words of praise. Psalm xvi. 6: "The lines are fallen unto me in pleasant places; yea, I have a *goodly* heritage." The psalmist means that through the maintenance of his lot by the kind providence of God he had come into a pleasant or beautiful station. Job xxvi. 13: "By His Spirit He hath *garnished* [or "beautified"] the heavens." Daniel iv. 2: "I thought it *good* [or "it seemed a seemly or beautiful thing to me"] to show the signs and wonders that the high God hath wrought toward me."

2. *More particular teaching of this station.*

The Hebrew word is also applied to the pleasant or clear sound of a trumpet, as in Exodus xix. 16. It is supposed by scholars that to this St. John refers when on the isle of Patmos he was led into a worshipful spirit by the sound of the clear trumpet (Rev. i. 10, iv. 1). When we truly worship God He talks to us with such clearness and persuasiveness as may be expressed by trumpet-tones; He leads us into truth and inspires us for battle.

3. *Comeliness of character comes through exaltation of thought and worship.*

It is to be observed that this place is called "Mount Shapher." It was a place of exaltation and wide prospects, teaching us that true worship lifts us above the external and sensible objects and brings us into a region of calm contemplation and vision. We are then able to understand the disciples' feeling when the Lord's face was transfigured before them on the mount (Matt. xxvii. 1–4); or we come into sympathy with Moses and Aaron, Nadab and Abihu, with the seventy elders, when "they saw the God of Israel:

and there was under His feet as it were a paved work of a sapphire stone, and as it were the body of heaven in his clearness" (Exod. xxiv. 1–11). In both of these cases the exaltation of soul resulted from sincere worship. The psalmist expresses the true idea of Shapher when he exclaims, "Worship the Lord in the *beauty* of holiness" (Ps. xxix. 2).

4. *Comeliness of character results from aloneness with God.*

It is when we are alone with God that He reveals to us the treasures of His love. It is when we go up into the mountain to Him that we understand His purposes. There, in silence, abstraction from the world, stillness of mind, and calmness of soul, we come close to the Father's heart. Daniel and Ezekiel were captives in Babylon when God revealed Himself so wonderfully to them. St. John was an exile on the isle of Patmos when the heavens were opened before his astonished vision. St. Paul went away into Arabia for three years, that the mysteries of the kingdom might be revealed to him; and even our Lord retired to the desert for forty days and resorted frequently to the mountain-tops to commune with God. What was it the Lord said unto Moses? "Look that thou make them [all things pertaining to the tabernacle] after their pattern, which was showed thee *in the mount*" (Exod. xxv. 40; cf. Heb. viii. 5). It was when Moses was alone with God on the mountain-top that the plan of the structure was shown him, and it is when we are alone with God on our spiritual Mount Shaphers that the plan of our life is unfolded to us. Frequently in our desert course let us resort thither!

5. *Obedience is also an element in comeliness of character.*

Look a moment at Psalm xxxiii. 1 : "Praise is comely for the upright." This seems to be almost a designed linking of the ideas of Kehelathah and Shapher—the station of worship and the station of beauty. Truly does real and devout praise to God produce comeliness in character by leading us to humility and obedience. We have about the same teaching in Psalm cxlvii. 1. Isaiah uses the word "Shapher" in connection with the appearance our blessed Lord should make in the eyes of men (Isa. liii. 2), to whom "He hath no form nor *comeliness.*" On the contrary, Ezekiel, in two passages of glorious import and beauty (xvi. 14, xvii. 10), declares that, though the natural man cannot see it, the *comeliness* of Jehovah God is radiant and infinite, and will be imparted to the faithful and obedient ones in all ages and even in heathen climes.

6. *Comeliness of character is attainable by all who will fulfil the conditions.*

The cheering prophecy of Isaiah (iv. 2) is: "In that day shall the branch of the Lord be beautiful and glorious, and the fruit [of the Spirit] on the earth shall be excellent and *comely.*" This is the real meaning. In all the "escaped ones" (or "saved") of Israel shall fruitage of love, joy, peace—all comely and blessed things—appear. Here we have the same Hebrew word and an unfolding of the thoughts which should possess us at this stage of our journey. Link with this the exhortation of the apostle in Philippians iv. 8: "Finally, brethren, whatsoever things are true, whatsoever things are honest, whatsoever things are just, whatsoever things are pure, whatsoever things are lovely, whatsoever things are of good report; if there be any virtue, and if there be any praise, think on these things." Let us thus endeavor to "adorn the doctrine." Oh, that our prayer may be, "Let the beauty of the Lord our God be upon us"! Oh, that we may be contented with nothing less than a comeliness of character that will attract men to the Christ who can impart such gifts unto His disciples!

There is nothing fair or glorious in the future life that may not be attained in part in this present life. We may now be kings and priests unto God, and be clad with the kingly and priestly robes of righteousness. We may now enter a heaven begun below (Deut. xi. 21), and taste at once its joys and sweets. The branches of the tree of life hang over the wall, and we may reach up and pluck of its leaves and fruits. Our "citizenship" may now "be in heaven," and thus may the "beauty of the Lord our God be upon us."

XXI

HARADAH

We cannot always remain on the mount. Like the peri, we must sometimes seem to turn away from the very gate of Paradise. There is a work to be done in the valley, and therefore we cannot make a permanent home on the blessed mount of transfiguration; we are not permitted even to build tabernacles there. But let us not forget that we may carry the transfigured face and the transfigured heart into the lowest life and duty. "Be not conformed to this world: but be ye transfigured" (Rom. xii. 2, Greek).

Reading on in the catalogue of the journeys in the wilderness, we come to this record: "And they removed from Mount Shapher, and encamped in Haradah" (Num. xxxiii. 24). We saw in our last study that "Shapher" means "comeliness." At that high station Israel enjoyed visions of God that bestowed beauty upon their characters and gave pleasantness to their hearts. Ah, what a change a few steps may make! "Haradah" means literally "great fear" or "trembling"; and it is into this sad plight that the length of a single verse conducted Israel. Do we not find here an apt type of what often befalls the soul? The mountain gives way to the valley, and spiritual exaltation is too often followed by depression and fear.

The Hebrew word from which "Haradah" comes is used in the following passages: Genesis xxvii. 33 ("trembled with a great trembling greatly," marg.), where the fear of Isaac is described when Esau, coming too late, found that his brother had obtained the blessing; Ezekiel xxvi. 16, where the trembling of ungodly princes is foretold; Exodus xix. 16, where Israel's fear before Sinai is mentioned; 1 Samuel xiii. 7, where the fears of Saul's people are described; 1 Samuel xiv. 15, where the wondrous story is told of the trembling that seized the hosts of the Philistines when Jonathan and his armor-bearer invaded them; and in Isaiah x. 29, where Ramah is declared to be afraid. These passages fully interpret the import of the name given to this desert station, and give us a clue to the mental and spiritual state of the Israelites. Does it seem strange to us that they should so soon fall from the exaltation of Shapher into the dejection of Haradah? Turn to Matthew's Gospel and see the wondrous change in even our Saviour's surroundings between the last verse of the third chapter and the first verse of the fourth. And see how Elijah, immediately after his splendid attitude and victory on Mount Carmel, casts himself down under a juniper-tree (1 Kings xix. 1–18).

There are three kinds of fear that may be studied with profit:

1. *The fear of conviction.*

What a trembling seizes the soul of man when a true sense of sin is brought home to his heart! Turn to 2 Kings vii. 3–7, and there find a true type of the fear that seizes the heart when God is near. These four leprous men were in the position occupied by the sinner. There was death behind them in the city from which they had come; there was death within them in two forms—hunger and leprosy; there was death before them in the army of the besieging enemy. So the sinner may have come a little way out of the City of Destruction; he may seem almost saved. But really he is altogether lost—death behind him, around him, within him, and before him. Oh, well if conviction of his state come to him and he say to himself and companions, "Why sit we here until we die?" Note that God took away the death that had been before them when the four lepers advanced. So does He take endless death out of our way and give us life when we obey His command to go forward. Oh, that there might be more direct and faithful preaching to the conscience!

2. *The fear of doubt.*

When Gideon was to select his army a proclamation was made that the fearful and trembling would be allowed to depart. The word "Haradah" is used in this passage (Judg. vii. 3). The meaning is that God needs men full of faith, who will not waver in battle. Even a little doubt weakens the whole man. God mentions this fear of doubt as part of punishment for past transgressions, as in that remarkable passage, Leviticus xxvi. 36. You will notice that Gideon's motley host had gathered at Harod (which is from the same root as "Haradah") when the fearful were to be eliminated (Judg. vii. 1). This name is as significant of the condition of Gideon's force as the word "Moreh" in the same passage is of the "rebellion" (for this is the meaning of the word "Moreh") of the Midianites. But Haradah hath its word of comfort also, as found in Isaiah lxvi. 2: "To this man will I look, even to him that is poor and of a contrite spirit, and *trembleth* at My word." What a blessed promise to those who feel themselves weak through doubt!

3. *The fear of conscientious service.*

This must be carefully distinguished from the fear of doubt. Many a sincere worker must say with Paul, "I was with you in weakness, and in fear, and in much trembling" (1 Cor. ii. 3). Yet this fear is honorable and right, and in no way to be confused with a doubting fear. Many a soul is troubled unnecessarily by losing sight of this distinction. Look also at 2 Corinthians vii. 15, and then see how the result of this conscientious trembling in view of great obligations insures skill in preaching Christ (2 Cor. v. 11) and brings comfort (2 Cor. i. 3–7).

It is well to note that God says twelve times in the Old Testament that no one shall make the truly godly afraid. The passages are: Leviticus xxvi. 6; Deuteronomy xxviii. 26; Job xi. 19; Isaiah xvii. 2; Jeremiah vii. 33, xxx. 10, xlvi. 27; Ezekiel xxxiv. 28, xxxix. 26; Micah iv. 4; Nahum ii. 11; Zephaniah iii. 13. In every instance the word is the root from which "Haradah" is derived.

That phase of fear which we call "worry" comes about because of partial faith or idleness in the Lord's vineyard. It puts us to the blush to notice how many of the persons mentioned in the Bible worried over ills that never came. Jacob was cast into despondency thinking Esau was coming against him in wrath, and also because he thought that Joseph was "without doubt rent in pieces." Both of these worriments were without foundation. Elijah worried because he thought he was the only faithful and godly man left upon the earth. His distress was altogether foolish, because, as God informed him, there were seven thousand others who had not bowed the knee to Baal. It was the same with David, Hezekiah, Jeremiah, and the disciples after Christ's death. It is the same now. Half the things we distress ourselves about will never happen to us, and God will turn the other half to our eternal profit.

But, blessed as is the teaching of the Old Testament for its reassuring of our trembling hearts, it is only when we come to the New Testament that fear is entirely done away. "Perfect love casteth out fear" (1 John iv. 18). We shall be calm in life, peaceful in death, and crowned with "boldness in the day of judgment" when our love for the Lord Jesus has become entire and absorbing. Oh, that the pierced hand may be laid upon every one of us, as upon John, and that we may hear the sweetest of all voices say, "Fear not"! (Rev. i. 17.)

XXII

MAKHELOTH

If there be dangers in the mountain-tops, so are there dangers to the travelers to Canaan in the valleys. We come to some of them now. The next verse of our chapter says, "And they removed from Haradah, and encamped in Makheloth." This latter name means literally "religious assemblies," a designation that would not, in itself, give any particular character to this station. When, however, we study all that happened to Israel there, we learn that there was a deep significance in this title, given, in deep misery, to their camping-place. And we ought to learn also something of spiritual value for our own warning. The sixteenth chapter of Numbers is supposed by Bromley and other scholars to describe what happened here at Makheloth. It is a picture of dissensions, rival assemblies, contentions in the congregation, and final disaster. For us the lessons are as to the duty of obeying the constituted authorities in the state and of cultivating a wide and charitable Christian unity in the church.

The assembling of ourselves together for divine worship is one of the most important duties of our desert journey. We know that Israel did not neglect it in the wilderness of Sinai. A short time ago we saw them at Kehelathah, which comes from the same Hebrew root as the name of the station we are now considering. It is singular in form, however, while "Makheloth" is plural. At the former station Israel united heartily together in worship of Jehovah, forming one grand, harmonious, tuneful congregation. They were then "with one accord in one place."

The solemn duty of church attendance is all too little regarded by the mass of professedly Christian people. The minister is supposed to be present, and certain of the officers, including the sexton. But the most frivolous of excuses are considered sufficient with the church-members. "Oh, I'm so tired," or, "My head aches to-day," or, "I've taken a little cold and I am afraid the rain will wet me, and I shall add to it." On these pleas men and women miss the wondrous privilege of meeting the Master face to face. Let us get it clearly established in our minds that church services are not primarily designed so that the pastor and sexton may earn their salaries or that the elders may show their fitness for reëlection to office, but that the power of the gospel may be brought to bear upon the hearts and lives of those who profess to love the Lord. To say nothing of the shame of leaving all the work to the pastor, it is the missing of a great privilege—the greatest that can be enjoyed on earth—to remain away from the place where the risen Christ has promised to meet His brethren. How much Thomas missed by absenting himself from one prayer-meeting! (John xx. 19–24.)

Let us take our Bibles, first of all, to see what frame of mind the worshiper should be in when approaching

God. We find that three things are insisted upon as necessary:

1. *Reverence toward God.*

This is the very first—the fundamental requisite. When "the Lord is in His holy temple," why should not "all the earth keep silence before Him"? (Hab. ii. 20.) Why should there be tittering and whispering and open eyes when the prayer is being offered? If, with the psalmist, we remembered that it is in the multitude of God's mercy that we come into His house, would we not "worship in fear toward His holy temple"? (Ps. v. 7. See also Ps. xxix. 2.) For all those who accept the New Testament as a rule of faith and practice, the Lord Jesus has settled the matter of reverential worship (John iv. 20–24). The Greek word translated "worship" in this passage is very expressive. It means "to kiss the hand toward," and is by far the most common word expressive of the idea of worship used in the New Testament. It is a strong oriental expression, containing the very essence of reverence. It is lovingly to "throw a kiss" toward God.

2. *Charity toward fellow-Christians.*

"As we forgive our debtors." "Leave there thy gift before the altar, . . . be reconciled, . . . then come and offer thy gift." The cold, unforgiving heart receives little benefit before the throne of grace. When we remember that the church service on earth is a type of the eternal service in heaven, how can we fail to understand that the same love should prevail here as there? See how our Lord speaks of it in Matthew viii. 11. This is a goodly fellowship indeed; and observe how the Lord links the present and the future in the word of absolute and gracious promise—"shall come." This goodly fellowship has five characteristics:

(*a*) It is a holy fellowship. Abraham, Isaac, and Jacob were holy men, and we must be holy if we wish to sit with them in heaven (Rev. vii. 14, xxi. 27).

(*b*) It is a multitudinous fellowship. "Many," says the Master (Rev. vii. 9).

(*c*) It is a diversified fellowship. They shall come from Asia, Africa, and America. Each one shall have his peculiar traits; but they shall be perfected and glorified (Luke xiii. 29).

(*d*) It is a familiar fellowship. Abraham shall be known as Abraham, and of the identity of Isaac and Jacob, Paul and Luther and Fénelon, there shall be no doubt (1 Cor. xiii. 12).

(*e*) It is an unbroken fellowship. We shall "sit down" with those who have obtained the victory. Here we are told to "move on!" Hurrying life and cruel destiny are the policemen that prevent us long obstructing the way. We are "Little Joes" here. We say, "Time flies;" but some one has wisely changed this into, "Time remains—we fly." And it is true. Time is always here, but we pass on. What a blessed thought it is that in heaven we shall be allowed to cultivate unbrokenly the friendships we so much prize here below!

If, then, this blessed fellowship shall be ours in the future, why not begin it here? Why not feel and manifest that love in our church assemblies and homes? If we would agree upon it there might be the same absence of criticism, the same kindly judgments, the same all-covering and all-helping charity.

3. *Humility toward ourselves.*

Pride is declared to be very like idolatry in worship (1 Sam. xv. 23). The only wise thing Ahab is reported to have said is (1 Kings xx. 11), "Let not him that girdeth on his harness boast himself as he that putteth it off." Our Saviour's first beatitude teaches humility (Matt. v. 3), and not long before His death He has the same lesson to teach (Matt. xxiii. 12). A blessed example of the humility of true worship we have in the case of Jacob, who bowed his head upon his staff (Heb. xi. 21).

As indicated above, it is supposed by many scholars that at Makheloth the children of Israel were disturbed by three princes, Korah, Dathan, and Abiram (Num. xvi. Study the chapter carefully). They sinned against God by denying Him the *reverence* due Him in worship. They sinned against Moses and all Israel by an *uncharitable* spirit, and against themselves and God as well, by *pride* and haughtiness. Hence they broke all the laws of true worship as we have studied them, and God gave them over to punishment. It is a singular coincidence, to say the least, that the name "Korah" literally means "ice" or "baldness," as if he were to stand for that spirit of unbelief which tends to harden the heart, destroy reverence to God, and despoil the life of its spiritual ornaments, as frost congeals and deprives the earth of its beauty and verdure. "Dathan" means "narrow law" or "narrowness," and he may represent that false spirit of uncharity which seems to imitate, but really opposes, the law of the spirit of life in Christ Jesus, which "sets free from the law of sin and death." "Abiram" signifies "the father of pride," and he represents the spirit of self-will which exalts itself against God's will and tempts us to do the same, thus destroying the humility pointed out above. So the very names of the leaders of this rebellion contain hints of the three sins committed by their followers, which same sins disturb the church to-day.

Uniformity in the means and methods of worship will probably be impossible and undesirable so long as human nature remains as it is. Denominations are a necessity of our complex being. But all who are following the leading of the one King through the desert should surely agree in that humble reverence which they owe to their Lord and that humble charity which they owe to one another. Oh, that all Christians alike might hear and heed the Master's saying, "If any man will come after Me, let him deny himself, and take up his cross daily, and follow Me"! (Luke ix. 23.) This is the true way of preserving us from the evils of Makheloth. A few stations back we saw how Moses asked Hobab to accompany them through the desert. We may learn a lesson from this, for the name "Hobab" signifies "love." It is a desirable thing that brotherly love go with us all through the desert, be "for eyes" to us, and a light unto our feet to preserve us from dangerous aberrations; for "he that loveth his brother abideth in the light, and there is none occasion of stumbling in him. But he that hateth his brother is in darkness, and walketh in darkness" (1 John ii. 10, 11).

XXIII

TAHATH

There is no lesson that the Christian has to learn so frequently in the desert experience as the need of humility. Israel was taught it at every step of their progress, and the child of God on the way to the heavenly Canaan needs to think of it and pray for it constantly. All outward circumstances help us, under the direction of divine Providence, to attain it. Disappointments come, failures attend our best-laid plans, inevitable sorrows and afflictions befall, the deaths of friends and loved ones startle us into sudden gravity and self-examination. All these and a thousand other providential dispensations teach us humility.

But there is one experience which above everything else impresses the lesson of our frailty upon us; that is, the falling into sin to which the best of us are liable. What can show the nothingness of human strength and the deceitfulness of the human heart so strongly as the sly and numerous sins to which we yield? This is the lesson of Tahath, the camping-place to which we have now come (Num. xxxiii. 26). For "Tahath" means "contrition" or "breaking," and coming directly after Makheloth, where Israel sinned, it shows the spiritual state of the people after they had witnessed God's judgment upon Korah, Dathan, and Abiram.

It is not difficult for us to form a mental picture of the Israelites as they journeyed from Makheloth to Tahath. They were still in the wilderness of Paran, and the dreariness of the dry and thirsty land stretched everywhere around them. Their heads were bowed and their hearts were sore, and their consciences troubled them. They had just seen fourteen thousand and seven hundred of their companions, besides them that died about the matter of Korah, swept away by the plague (Num. xvi. 49). What an awful scene it must have been! No wonder they go along now through the wilderness with their heads bowed like the bulrushes. How many of them had really understood the significance of Aaron's attitude and action when he took a censer and put fire therein and ran down quickly to make an atonement? (Num. xvi. 46.) How many had faith to discern the work of the coming Messiah in this event? Let us hope a great many.

At our spiritual Tahath we may learn three lessons:

1. *Contrition has a relation to sin, but there is a proviso.*

Genuine contrition is always a good trait, but Christians should not wait to manifest it until God has shown them by signal judgments how strong is His hatred of sin. I do not say that the repentance which results from fear is always spurious; but there should always be an element of faith in contrition. Our fear of self should be linked with holy confidence in God. The divine "goodness" should "lead us to repentance."

There are two very strong words used in the Old Testament to express contrition. One means "to be smitten," and is used in Isaiah lxvi. 2: "To this man will I look, even to him that is poor and of a contrite [smitten] spirit, and trembleth at My word." The other means "to be bruised," and is used in the following passages: Psalm xxxiv. 18: "Saveth such as be of a *contrite* spirit;" Isaiah lvii. 15: "With him also that is of a *contrite* . . . spirit;" and Psalm li. 17. "A broken and a *contrite* heart." This last verse is a very beautiful one. The Hebrew word translated "broken" is the root of our word "shivered,"—i.e., "broken to atoms,"—so that the verse should read, " A shivered and bruised heart, O God, Thou wilt not despise." Such a heart would be completely emptied of self, because so broken that it could contain none.

2. *Contrition has a relation to humility; the thoughts differ only slightly.*

We are apt to use the words "humility" and "contrition" in very different senses. We speak of the latter as being the necessary feeling of an aroused, impenitent person; we speak of the former as a Christian virtue. Are we not in danger of running into error in this way? Contrition is simply that humility which results from a strong sense of sin. It is as much a Christian grace as a necessity for the impenitent. In the Bible the words "humility" and "humiliation" are constant and interchangeable. Notice how, in the following fifteen passages, these ideas are linked together: Deuteronomy viii. 2, xxi. 14, xxii. 24, 29; Psalm xxxv. 13; Daniel v. 22; Luke xiv. 11; 2 Corinthians xii. 21; 2 Kings xxii. 19; 2 Chronicles vii.

14; Exodus v. 3; Jeremiah xiii. 18; Leviticus xxvi. 41; Colossians iii. 12; 1 Peter v. 6.

While it is true that to the extent that we abide in Christ we are free from sin, yet we are always being swept off our feet by sudden temptation, or we find ourselves drifting into unknown sin. Hence the need of constant watchfulness and frequent repentance even to Christians. If we walk in the light, "the blood of Jesus Christ is cleansing us constantly from sin" (1 John i. 7, Greek). We may be conscious that we are being washed each moment from the sin of that moment. And so a feeling of sadness, of contrition, because of our frailty, must mingle with the thanksgiving and praise with which we acknowledge the application of the blood.

There is a very instructive passage as to the daily washing away of evil in John xiii. 1–10: Jesus girded Himself with a towel and washed the disciples' feet. He came to Peter, and that disciple said, "Thou shalt never wash my feet." Jesus said, "If I wash thee not, thou hast no part with Me." Then the impulsive disciple cried beseechingly, "Lord, not my feet only, but also my hands and my head." Then the Master lays down the all-important principle of the daily cleansing of those who once have been washed in His blood. "Jesus saith to him, He that hath *taken a bath* needeth not save to wash his feet, but is clean every whit." When one steps out of the bath and goes out sandaled to walk the streets, he soils only his feet; and so the Master implies that, as we go about our daily tasks having once for all been cleansed in His blood, we have but to bring to Him at nightfall the part of our nature that has become defiled. This He will cleanse, and so, ere we rest, we shall be cleansed every whit. What a comforting reflection! And how interesting to notice that Peter never forgot this scene. When writing his first letter to the brethren he gives us a vivid and practical word of advice, drawing a simile from what he had seen his Lord do. "Tie on humility as a garment," he says (1 Pet. v. 5, Greek). As Jesus girded Himself with the towel in token of His willingness to take a servant's place, so we should bind ourselves with humility in view of the number of times we need to come to Jesus to have the soiled part of our natures recleansed. Oh, indeed, as Peter goes on, we ought to humble ourselves "under the mighty hand of God, that He may exalt" us in due season (verse 6).

3. *Contrition has a relation to the divine mercy, which should by no means be forgotten.*

It is interesting to note that Ezekiel prophesies three times (vi. 10, xx. 43, xxxvi. 31) that Israel should be led to contrition through the mercy of God. Mercies at Jerusalem shall do what all the judgments at Babylon could not accomplish. So has it always been. Study the lives of the great patriarchs and see how they loathed sin because they loved God's smile. Moses (in Deuteronomy entire), Job (in the end of his book—xl. 4, xlii. 6), David (in the penitential psalms as well as 2 Sam. xii. 13), St. Peter (in the Gospel of Mark, written under his direction and describing his faults vividly), and St. Paul (in his frequent descriptions of his fanatical zeal before his conversion—Acts xxii. 3-20; 1 Cor. xv. 9, etc.) are all examples. David's love melted Saul's heart, Christ's reproachful look sent

Peter to his flood of penitential tears, and the mercy of God shining out of heaven upon our hearts makes them mourn in contrition. See the wondrously beautiful simile in 2 Corinthians vii. 7. The word "mourning" means the passionate cry of parent birds when robbed of their young. So Homer uses the Greek word. The mourning for iniquity is also compared to the plaintive and melancholy notes of doves of the valley (Ezek. vii. 16); but there is a stronger figure still. In Zechariah xii. 10 it is said, "They shall look upon Me whom they have pierced, and they shall mourn for Him, as one mourneth for his only son, and shall be in bitterness for Him, as one that is in bitterness for his first-born." Oh, what deep and moving grief! It is no longer the grief of birds and doves, but of heart-broken father and mother. May the Holy Spirit awaken some such self-humiliation in all those who have sinned, so that they and we may attend to the sweet counsel of Jesus: "Take My yoke upon you and learn of Me; for I am meek and lowly in heart: and ye shall find rest unto your souls" (Matt. xi. 29).

XXIV

TARAH

THE Israelites had once been at Elim, it is to be remembered, where God gave them refreshment after the severities of the desert journeyings. We have had a full description of Elim, with its palms and fountains. It was one of those delightfully refreshing oases that travelers sometimes happen on in parched and dusty deserts. But of Tarah we have no description save what the name itself contains. Yet this station was a second Elim to the thirsty and fatigued travelers. God mercifully gave it to them that their souls might rejoice. What they enjoyed there is revealed in the name of the station, for "Tarah" means "breathing" or "respite." This is the very essence of refreshment in a parched wilderness. A long breath under shady trees, with the sound of cool waters near, is what the traveler pants for, and, receiving, blesses God and takes courage.

Nor was the refreshment entirely physical. At Tahath, as we saw in our last study, they had deeply humbled themselves before God. Ah, the step from Tahath to Tarah, how short, how glorious! True and "godly sorrow worketh repentance to salvation not to be repented of" (2 Cor. vii. 10). Not one Israelite repented of the step that led him to Tarah. They had humbled themselves, and God lifted them up; they had breathed forth contrition, and God led them to the breathing-place of respite and delight.

There is even more than this in the name of our station. Along with the "breathing" is an idea of "smelling," and, more generally, the "perception of spiritual things through the senses." Bible students must not overlook this in the Word. St. John means something when he begins his first epistle with the words, "That which we have heard, which we have seen with our eyes, which we have looked upon, and our hands have handled, of the Word of life." He means more than that Thomas had been allowed to thrust his hand into Christ's side, and that he himself had been encouraged to "lean back upon" that divine breast. (See the fine contrast in the Greek between "reclining next Christ," John xiii. 23, and "leaning back on Jesus' breast," verse 25, when there was a tender question to be asked.) John means to indicate the spiritual joy and knowledge of truth which often come to the child of God through the thrill of the senses. The Sabbath bell, the sight of the misty mountains, the Christian hand-clasp, may be the means of grace and growth. What does the church sing of Christ? "All Thy garments smell of myrrh, and aloes, and cassia" (Ps. xlv. 8). In this figure are shown the delights of Tarah. And here we see the explanation of that hard saying in Isaiah xi. 3: "The Spirit of the Lord shall make him of quick *scent* [marg.]

in the fear of the Lord," etc. The word italicized is a translation of a Hebrew word derived from "Tarah." The word sets forth the quick spiritual perception with which Christ was endowed. "He knew what was in man." He did not need to "judge after the sight of His eyes, neither reprove after the hearing of His ears." The breathing in of the "joy of the Lord" endows the Christian also with exalted knowledge of the world's nature and the heart's needs, and God's fullness of supply.

How kind and merciful God is to give us breathing-places in the wilderness journey! The whole gospel is full of joy, but these stations are added drops. See how Isaiah uses such resting-places as Tarah to show forth the refreshment of divine truth (Isa. xxxv. 1–7. This seventh verse is often misunderstood. "The parched ground" is literally "the serab," i.e., the mirage of the desert. The meaning is, "This unsubstantial semblage of water shall become a real pool." Fictitious, worldly joys shall to the Christian be displaced by real and permanent peace and refreshment).

Is it not a significant fact that Christ's first miracle was turning water into wine? Water was a type of sorrow. In tears it was shed, in penitence it was poured out before the Lord. Wine has always been the type of joy (Ps. civ. 15; Cant. i. 2; Isa. xxv. 6; Zech. x. 7). John well says, therefore, that the first miracle of Christ "manifested forth His glory." For what is the Messiah's glory if it be not to change the sins and sorrows of His children into heavenly joy? How many a tried Christian has been constrained to say to the Saviour, when the severest woes have been changed to blessings, "Thou hast kept the good wine until now"! In the hour of death this thankful phrase will be upon our lips with double meaning.

May we not learn here at Tarah what the apostle (Heb. v. 14) means by "senses" that are so "exercised by habit" (marg.) that they discern good and evil? While we enjoy God-given respites, let us grow to that "perfection" that will enable us to take the "strong meat" of the Word.

And here at Tarah let us take a deep inbreathing of the Holy Spirit. He is the living breath of the living God. To *in*spire is to breathe *in*, to live; to *ex*pire is to breathe *out*, to die. The inspired writers and workers in all ages are those who have *breathed in* the Holy Spirit. How significant that Jesus "breathed on the disciples" and said to them, "Receive ye the Holy Ghost" (John xx. 22). Let us take time to go away by ourselves frequently, that we may take deep, thoughtful, blessed inhalations of the Spirit. Our soul's health depends upon it. No valuable service can be rendered without it. So shall we have the Tarah experience on our journey to Canaan.

The Christian will not have come all the way from Rameses to Tarah on the way to heaven without being filled with the Holy Spirit. The consecration, worship, contrition, and growth we have been considering all imply it. However, some who read these pages may not be distinctly conscious of the reception of the Holy Spirit. Let me set down three things in regard to it—things which many have written about and which may be perfectly familiar to most Christian students.

1. *Every believer ought to be filled with the Holy Ghost, and therefore may be so filled.*

Acts ii. 4 says, "They were all filled," though men and women were there, and not all of them were called officially to be pastors and missionaries. In an account of a similar enduement occurring subsequently (Acts iv. 31) the same words are used; "all" were filled. If the duty be not paramount there is no force in the injunction to the Ephesians, which also belongs to us (Eph. v. 18): "Be filled with the Spirit."

2. *But not every believer is filled.*

The facts of the case are mournful in the extreme. Many Christians fail to show the marks of being filled with the Spirit. These marks, as indicated in Acts ii. 46, 47, are: (1) delight in God's house, in Christian fellowship; (2) gladness, Christian joy pervading the whole life; (3) a spirit of praise. Acts iv. 31 adds to these: (4) boldness in speaking the Word; (5) unity of spirit; (6) actual love for each other manifested by unselfishness; (7) power in witnessing for Jesus; (8) great grace upon them all. To these let Galatians v. 22 be added, and we have: (9) the exhibition in a marked degree of the Christian virtues there named. The reasons why many Christians are not filled with the Spirit are not hard to find.

(*a*) Some grieve the Spirit (Eph. iv. 30). This is done by inconsistency in the life.

(*b*) Some quench the Spirit (1 Thess. v. 19). The life may be consistent, but there is a neglect of the Word and sacraments, of private Bible study and prayer; or the cares and pleasures of this life fill the heart, and the Spirit is crowded out; or it may be simply that with earnest desires and prayers there is a failure to use the power; and it is given for use (1 Cor. vii. 7), not for feelings of joy and rapture.

(c) Some resist the Spirit (Isa. lxiii. 10). They take up arms of rebellion; they will not be ruled by Him. He says, "Go into the ministry," or, "Go to the foreign field," or, "Take this humble post," or, "Have the family prayer in your home;" and the man says, "I know I ought to, BUT—" and he will not.

3. *The seven steps to be taken* by every one who would be filled have been drawn from the Bible, and are as follows:

(a) Enthrone Jesus (John vii. 39).

(b) Repent of sin (Acts ii. 38).

(c) Openly confess Christ; "be baptized" (Acts ii. 38).

(d) Determine to obey God fully and cheerfully (Acts v. 32).

(e) Desire the filling (Luke xi. 13).

(f) Definitely ask for the filling (Luke xi. 13).

(g) Receive by faith (Gal. iii. 14).

Take a few moments and see if you can quietly and heartily take these seven steps. Then take a deep inhalation of the Spirit into your soul. Then "reckon" that you have Him to abide in you forever.

XXV

MITHCAH

EARLY in their journey Israel had been led to Marah, "bitterness." Now they are led to Mithcah, "sweetness" (Num. xxxiii. 28). There was a weary journey between the two stations, but was not the joy worth all the trial? At Mithcah the weary travelers enjoyed the sweet communion with God that removes the remembrance of all that has passed before. Indeed, the word from which "Mithcah" is taken occurs in Exodus xv. 25, where it is said that a tree was cast into the waters of Marah and they became "sweet." Mithcah is the antidote to Marah literally and figuratively. They who stand upon the sea of glass in the Father's home remember no more the great tribulations out of which they have come. In like manner, Israel and the Christian are freed from the terrors of Haradah and the contrition of Tahath when they come to the sweetness of Mithcah. How many times in the journey to the promised Canaan the child of God is led into "large places" of praise (Ps. xxxi. 8) and to stations of sweetness, where the desert is forgotten and God becomes all and in all!

It seems probable that the incidents recorded in the

seventeenth chapter of Numbers occurred at this station. If so a double significance and beauty will be given to the secret locked within the name. God was anxious that the murmurings of the Israelites should entirely cease (Num. xvii. 5). He determines to give them one more sign. He had been more than kind to them before, but the great love wherewith He loved them prompted Him to add sign upon sign. Oh, never did a father pity his children as our God pities us! So the Lord directed that a representative of each tribe should bring a rod into the tabernacle of the congregation. Moses was to take them and lay them in place before the ark of testimony, and God promised to meet with him there and show him something wonderful. It was done. Among the rest was a rod brought by Aaron, who represented the tribe of Levi. And lo! on the morrow the rod of Aaron "was budded, and brought forth buds, and bloomed blossoms, and yielded almonds" (verse 8). Picture the wondrous miracle! Out of the dead, black, apparently useless staff there came the beautiful fragrant blossoms and the lovely refreshing almonds. Life came out of death; beauty came out of black and commonplace ugliness; sweetness came out of sapless strands of fiber. No wonder this place was called Mithcah, "sweetness"! No wonder this rod was kept in the ark of the covenant (Heb. ix. 4) as a testimony against any further murmuring; no wonder it became a symbol of strength and miraculous blessing! (Ps. cx. 2; Ezek. xix. 12–14.)

The word "Mithcah" is often used in the Bible; it is sometimes applied to natural bodies that are sweet to the taste, as figs (Judg. ix. 11). Sometimes it is used of physical enjoyments, as the sleep of the laboring man (Eccles. v. 12) and the pleasures of secret sin (Prov. ix. 17). But the word is also employed of high and noble enjoyments which the Christian may well covet. Look up and study carefully the following, in which the root word occurs: Judges xiv. 18; Nehemiah viii. 10; Proverbs xvi. 24; Ecclesiastes xi. 7; Song of Solomon ii. 3; Isaiah v. 20; Job xxi. 33. To seven particular things let us pay attention.

1. *Counsel.*

Whether from man or God, true counsel is sweet. Psalm lv. 14: "We took sweet counsel together, and walked into the house of God in company;" Proverbs xvi. 21: "The wise in heart shall be called prudent: and the sweetness of the lips increaseth learning." It is a blessed thing to have a friend in whose judgment we may trust and with whom we may exchange advice and consolation. And there is a best Friend of all, who sticketh closer than a brother.

2. *Meditation.*

The psalmist cries, "My meditation of Him shall be sweet" (Ps. civ. 34). To a pure and godly mind there can be no solitude. God is always present, holy thoughts and emotions are always nigh, and the Christian can surround and fill himself with the divine sweetness of pious meditation. What a blessing it is that we can drink in calmly, quietly, the sweet breaths of the divine Spirit, who is glad to show Himself under the figure of freshly blowing breezes of the springtime! (John iii. 8.)

3. *The Word.*

David understood what sweetness is, and does not hesitate to say (Ps. cxix. 103), "How sweet are Thy words unto my taste! yea, sweeter than honey to my mouth." The Christian likewise dwells upon the teachings of the Word with constant and growing delight. "And Jesus said unto them, I am the bread of life: he that cometh to Me shall never hunger; and he that believeth on Me shall never thirst" (John vi. 35); "Thy words were found, and I did eat them; and Thy word was unto me the joy and rejoicing of mine heart: for I am called by Thy name, O Lord God of hosts" (Jer. xv. 16); "Neither have I gone back from the commandment of His lips; I have esteemed the words of His mouth more than my necessary food" (Job xxiii. 12); "Blessed are they which do hunger and thirst after righteousness: for they shall be filled" (Matt. v. 6).

4. *Judgments.*

"Sweeter also than honey and the honeycomb," says David, are the "judgments of the Lord" (Ps. xix. 10). By judgments I understand all the decisions of God in providence and grace, as well as all the conclusions of His mind as to our welfare. Truly they are sweet to the one who can say, "Not my will, but Thine, be done."

5. *Believing.*

"Peace in believing" (Rom. xv. 13). What a beautiful thought! The wife has peace in believing that the husband is true to her; the child has peace in believing that the mother's breast is its proper pillow. There is a sweetness in childlike trust in God that makes all other joys seem trivial.

6. *Communion.*

" Did not our heart burn within us, while He opened to us the Scriptures? " said the two disciples at Emmaus (Luke xxiv. 32). The word here rendered "burn" means "to boil"—to be *boiling hot.* It is the same word we have in Revelation iii. 15 : " I would thou wert *hot.*" Our Lord wants us to be boiling in fervor and love. No one has such sweetness of temper and life as he who is in earnest for the Master. Delightful communion does our risen Lord offer to all His brethren who will walk with Him.

7. *The love of God.*

Truly this is sweet. "The love of God is shed abroad in our hearts by the Holy Ghost," says Paul, in Romans v. 5. What ineffable sweetness is here! " Oh, taste and see that the Lord is good." Cheer the wilderness journey by opening the heart to the love of God, which He is so willing to *shed,* diffuse copiously, into and all through it.

XXVI

HASHMONAH

Moving on from the sweet enjoyments of Mithcah, the people came to a station called Hashmonah, and pitched there (Num. xxxiii. 29). We are coming to very sacred and holy ground now. Aaron, the high priest, becomes the central figure, taking precedence even of Moses in the sublime picture. This is because we are coming toward Mount Hor. On this mountain Aaron died, under circumstances which have awed and instructed the world, and awe and instruct us still. He was an example of a man growing richer in experience and more useful in service as he approached the end of his life. What a noble thing it is to find gray hairs in the way of righteousness! The world applauds the patriarch in political and national affairs who is able to work on until he has reached fourscore years. And surely the angels must rejoice when they see Christian standard-bearers who preserve inward youth, cheerfulness, adaptability, and faithfulness even to the end of life.

Notice that God, in the eighteenth and nineteenth chapters of Numbers, addresses His commands directly to Aaron. The law for the maintenance of the priests is to be declared, and so God speaks to the high priest face to face. Hitherto He had spoken mostly through Moses; but Aaron was now coming into very close and blessed relations with Jehovah. All his envy of Moses had been put away; the sign of the budding rod had been given him; he was being prepared for Mount Hor. It is sweet to see a man or woman ripening for heaven. The dear Lord often carries on the work of sanctification with rapidity and with special movings of grace at the end. We should rejoice in this, as it is a sign of infinite love and a promise and prophecy of infinite blessedness.

But, though Aaron was progressing rapidly in the divine life, we find that the Israelites were falling now and again into very distressing sins. We have no detailed account of what occurred at Hashmonah, but we can legitimately draw from the meaning of the word that the people here took a backward step. "Hashmonah" means literally "a hasty numbering." The station would be very impressive to the Jew, much more so than to us.

For this haste must be understood not as that occasioned by fear of the nearness of enemies, but by presumption. Scholars tell us that the word contains the idea of chaffing talk, of loud boasting, of that pleasurable bantering which a company of soldiers might engage in before a battle in which success was assured. It was the boasting which he who "girds on his armor" was accustomed to indulge in. It was the sarcastic challenge of self-sufficiency which Goliath hurled against David.

The people of Israel, made proud by the sweet refreshment of the last station, took a census of the forces they could command, with a view to fighting their own way into Canaan. Their privilege led them to presumption. How vividly have we seen all the way along the unevenness of the Israelites' life, now up and now down, in constant change! But are our feelings any more firm, our sentiments any more steady, and our course any more constant? Marah leads to Elim, and Mithcah to Hashmonah.

1. The lesson for the Christian is plain. By all means avoid presumption; let not despair drive you to it, let not privilege lead you to it. David numbered the people presumptuously, and God destroyed seventy thousand of them to humble him (2 Sam. xxiv.). Gideon might have boasted in the number of his army, and God taught him that three hundred willing and active ones alone were to be chosen (Judg. vii. 6). All this pointed the Jew back to Hashmonah, where Israel sinned by numbering the people, and it may well turn our memories to the same spot. On presumption study the following passages: Psalm lxxv. 5; Isaiah iii. 16; Proverbs xvii. 19; Job xxxviii. 11; Hosea v. 5; 2 Peter ii. 18; Jude 16.

2. Another lesson for us to learn is this: let us avoid hasty estimates. Study the world before you desire its pleasures or estimate too highly its promises. Know a person thoroughly before passing an estimate upon his character. Be very careful of giving judgments on the times in which you live, as if the spirit of Elias had come and incarnated in you "to restore all things" (Matt. xvii. 11). The deliverer to turn away ungodliness may not have appeared in your day (Rom.

xi. 26). The disciples were often wrong on this point, looking always for a restoration of an earthly kingdom to Israel (Acts i. 6).

3. In one other respect the hasty numbering may yield us practical lessons. We are not to try to decide when the great prophecies are to be fulfilled. The year 1666 was set as the time for the overthrow of the Roman hierarchy; 1881 was supposed by many to be the limit of the world's existence. The times and seasons are in God's hand; He is "the wonderful numberer," or "numberer of secrets" (Dan. viii. 13, marg. See Acts i. 7). Let us leave the matter with Him. We are commanded to watch. This implies that the time of the Lord's coming and the details of the consummation of all things are uncertain.

In general the spiritual lesson of this station is that we are often tempted to fix our eyes upon outward instead of inward things. Statistics dazzle us. We pin our faith in the Lord's power to save the world upon the number of converts reported by the several Christian denominations. These may be assurances in a general way that Christ is moving upon the hearts of men; but our belief in His power and wisdom should be founded upon something deeper than mere numberings of secretaries. Above all things let us keep the eye fixed upon the Master, who shall "see the travail of His soul, and be satisfied." Let us be sure that we are doing our part, by inward yieldings and by outward service, to hasten His coming.

XXVII

MOSEROTH

LIFE is a succession of lights and shades. The Christian's life is an alternating discipline of joys and sorrows, favors and afflictions. The number of the desert stations where Israel was afflicted must have been noticed by the student who has followed this series; but there was not one more than was needed; there was not one without a cause in their own conduct; there was not one which was not matched by a station where God showed His face in mercy and favor to His wandering children. Under these circumstances the shadows but proved the strength of the light; the chastisement became an evidence of a fatherly love.

In Moseroth, our next station (Num. xxxiii. 30), we have all of these ideas brought out. The word may mean either "bonds," "chastisements," or "instructions." In the light of the last station these meanings become very important. At Hashmonah the Israelites were guilty of hasty and petulant numbering of their soldiers, as if to go to war in their own strength. For this sin God punished them, and the station where the punishment fell upon them they called Moseroth, or "chastisements." The root from which this name comes is used in Psalm xciv. 12: "Blessed is the man whom Thou *chastenest*, O Lord;" and in Proverbs xxix. 15: "The rod and *reproof* give wisdom."

What the particular afflictions were that befell them at this station we are not told. That they were brought on by disobedience is plain; that they were nevertheless expressive of the Father's love is sure. Israel might gladly welcome them, though by no means "joyous"; for "afterward" they yielded the "peaceable fruit of righteousness."

It is significant that "Moseroth" means either "chastisements" or "instructions"; for the divine correction imparts true knowledge to those who are "exercised thereby"—knowledge of God, of the divine law, of sin and its punishment. To show the importance of the idea contained in the root word from which "Moseroth" comes, look at the following passages, in all of which it occurs:

1. Translated "bond" or "bonds": "He looseth the bond of kings, and girdeth their loins with a girdle" (Job xii. 18); "O Lord, truly I am Thy servant; I am Thy servant, and the son of Thine handmaid: Thou hast loosed my bonds" (Ps. cxvi. 16); "I will get me unto the great men, and will speak unto them; for they have known the way of the Lord, and the judgment of their God: but these have altogether broken the yoke, and burst the bonds" (Jer. v. 5); "Thus saith the Lord to me; Make thee bonds and yokes, and put them upon thy neck" (Jer. xxvii. 2); "For it shall come to pass in that day, saith the Lord of hosts, that I will break his yoke from off thy neck, and will burst

thy bonds, and strangers shall no more serve themselves of him" (Jer. xxx. 8); "And I will cause you to pass under the rod, and I will bring you into the bond of the covenant" (Ezek. xx. 37); "For now will I break his yoke from off thee, and will burst thy bonds in sunder" (Nah. i. 13).

2. Translated "chasten" or "chastisement": "And know ye this day: for I speak not with your children which have not known, and which have not seen the chastisement of the Lord your God, His greatness, His mighty hand, and His stretched-out arm" (Deut. xi. 2); "Behold, happy is the man whom God correcteth: therefore despise not thou the chastening of the Almighty" (Job v. 17); "I have heard the check [chastisement] of my reproach, and the spirit of my understanding causeth me to answer" (Job xx. 3); "Surely it is meet to be said unto God, I have borne chastisement, I will not offend any more" (Job xxxiv. 31); "My son, despise not the chastening of the Lord; neither be weary of His correction" (Prov. iii. 11); "He that spareth his rod hateth his son: but he that loveth him chasteneth him betimes" (Prov. xiii. 24); "Lord, in trouble have they visited Thee; they poured out a prayer when Thy chastening was upon them" (Isa. xxvi. 16); "He was wounded for our transgressions, He was bruised for our iniquities: the chastisement of our peace was upon Him; and with His stripes we are healed" (Isa. liii. 5); "All thy lovers have forgotten thee; they seek thee not; for I have wounded thee with the wound of an enemy, with the chastisement of a cruel one, for the multitude of thine iniquity; because thy sins were increased" (Jer. xxx. 14).

3. Translated "instruction": "Then He openeth the ears of men, and sealeth their instruction" (Job xxxiii. 16); "Seeing thou hatest instruction, and castest My words behind thee" (Ps. l. 17); "But they obeyed not, neither inclined their ear, but made their neck stiff, that they might not hear, nor receive instruction" (Jer. xvii. 23); "And they have turned unto Me the back, and not the face: though I taught them, rising up early and teaching them, yet they have not hearkened to receive instruction" (Jer. xxxii. 33); "Thus saith the Lord of hosts, the God of Israel; Go and tell the men of Judah and the inhabitants of Jerusalem, Will ye not receive instruction to hearken to My words? saith the Lord" (Jer. xxxv. 13); "So it shall be a reproach and a taunt, an instruction and an astonishment unto the nations that are round about thee, when I shall execute judgments in thee in anger and in fury and in furious rebukes. I the Lord have spoken it" (Ezek. v. 15); "I said, Surely thou wilt fear Me, thou wilt receive instruction; so their dwelling should not be cut off, howsoever I punished them: but they rose early, and corrupted all their doings" (Zeph. iii. 7). Besides these, observe that in Proverbs the word is used twenty-four times and translated "instruction."

4. It is worthy of remark that a Greek word (*paiduo*) used frequently in the New Testament contains the same ideas of "chastisement" and "instruction." Note the following: "But when we are judged, we are chastened of the Lord, that we should not be condemned with the world" (1 Cor. xi. 32); "As unknown, and yet well known; as dying, and, behold, we live; as

chastened, and not killed" (2 Cor. vi. 9); "All Scripture is given by inspiration of God, and is profitable for doctrine, for reproof, for correction, for instruction in righteousness" (2 Tim. iii. 16); "As many as I love, I rebuke and chasten: be zealous therefore, and repent" (Rev. iii. 19). Study carefully Hebrews xii. 5–11, and note how in every verse the subject is treated of under all aspects. In all of these the word is *paiduo*, which itself comes from the word meaning "boy" or "child." As chastisement and instruction are implied in the right development of every child, so are they needed in the education of the child of God.

XXVIII

BENE-JAAKAN

THE correction administered to Israel at Moseroth was continued in their next station, which received the name of Bene-jaakan (Num. xxxiii. 31). This name signifies "the children of great tribulation." It comes from a Hebrew word which means "to press" or "to squeeze," as a cart is pressed that is heavy laden. In this sense it is used in Amos ii. 13: "Behold, I am pressed under you, as a cart is pressed that is full of sheaves." It is used in the sense of oppression in Psalm lv. 3: "Because of the voice of the enemy, because of the oppression of the wicked: for they cast iniquity upon me, and in wrath they hate me." These passages show how wonderfully significant was the name given to this camping-place in the desert, where, in the midst of the divine chastisements, they called themselves "the children of great pressure" or "tribulation." Our Saviour uses an expression precisely analogous to this when He says, "But I have a baptism to be baptized with; and how am I *straitened* [i.e., "pressed" or "afflicted"] till it be accomplished!" (Luke xii. 50.) The same idea and the same Greek words are found in Acts xviii. 5, where Paul was "pressed in the spirit," wishing to testify for Christ. Again, in 2 Corinthians vi. 12, Paul charges the Christians in Corinth with being "straitened" or "pressed" in their affection for him. Other Old Testament instances of the use of the Hebrew word are: "The steps of his strength shall be straitened, and his own counsel shall cast him down" (Job xviii. 7); "When thou goest, thy steps shall not be straitened; and when thou runnest, thou shalt not stumble" (Prov. iv. 12); "For they were in three stories, but had not pillars as the pillars of the courts: therefore the building was straitened more than the lowest and the middlemost from the ground" (Ezek. xlii. 6); "O thou that art named The house of Jacob, is the Spirit of the Lord straitened? are these His doings? do not My words do good to him that walketh uprightly?" (Micah ii. 7.)

There is something further to be said in explanation of the name of this station. There was at that time a small tribe or clan called Bene-jaakan. They were sons of Jaakan, as their names implied, and Jaakan was descended from Seir the Horite (1 Chron. i. 38–42). They seem to have had their home in the valleys and fastnesses around Mount Hor, to the eastward of the desert of Zin, in which the people were now journeying. Seir signifies "hairy," "a goat," "a satyr," "a devil," and he seems to have been of the stock of Canaan (Gen. xxxvi. 20, 21, 27). All this was very bad, and the Israelites, who knew these names and the history of the individuals so well, could not have taken a more humiliating name for their station in the wilderness than Bene-jaakan. It conveyed to their minds a vivid idea of the connection between sin and punishment. It attested their own humility and desire to avoid in the future the sins which had been so ruinous to the clan whose name they used for their stopping-place. Moses speaks of the "children of Jaakan" in Deuteronomy x. 6 in a way to show that their characteristics were well known to the Israelites.

1. We learn here, first of all, something of the power of influence. In the margin of the passage in 1 Chronicles referred to above you will find that Jaakan was another name for Achan. Now it must not be supposed that the Achan who afterward troubled Israel is the person here meant. He was an Israelite, while the Jaakan of the text was a descendant of Canaan. But it might have been that there had been an admixture of races, or at least an admixture of influences between the races, so that bad blood and bad life in Israel resulted. Influence is one of the strongest forces in the universe, and the "troubler of Israel" may have owed his defection and deceit, if not his very name, to the Achan who was a dweller in the valleys around Mount Hor. Certain it is that the similarity in names and characters is most significant, and it may well lead us to think upon the influence we are exerting and the influences under which we are conscious of living. Such a little thing may lead us away from the dear Lord and make us deceivers and troublers!

2. Another lesson for us is that it is sometimes necessary for God to add one station of affliction to another in order to bring us to a proper humility. Moseroth was not enough for Israel. It is often insufficient for us, and we must be led to deeper sorrows and more telling chastisements. How much better to submit our

wills quickly, gladly, to the divine will! Even the world says that "it never rains but it pours." Paul speaks of "sorrow upon sorrow," but, thank God, he also speaks of "abundance of grace," while St. John promises "grace for grace." Let us never forget, even when the afflictions are deepening, that "whom the Lord loveth He chasteneth." And when the severest tests are applied let us remember that the fire is sent not in cursing, but in blessing, as in the promise (Isa. xlviii. 10, marg.): "Behold, I have refined thee, but not for silver; I have chosen thee in the furnace of affliction." (Compare Ezek. xxii. 20, 22.)

It is very interesting to observe how a common idea of pressure or crushing runs through all the world's thought of affliction. Take our word "tribulation." It contains the simile of "threshing." As under the strokes of the flail the precious grains of wheat are separated from the chaff, so under the rod of tribulation the wholesome graces of character are brought to the light, and the refuse is left to be scattered by the winds. We speak also of the "wine" of life, but this implies the crushing of many ripened grapes and the outflowing of the mingled richness. All of these similes remind us of the pressing sorrows through which God at Bene-jaakan led His people to the "peaceable fruit of righteousness."

XXIX

HOR-HAGIDGAD

IF the reader has closely followed the passages thus far he must be impressed with the wonderful analogy between the journeys of Israel in the desert and the inward experiences of the Christian on the way to the heavenly Canaan. The youngest followers of Christ must have gained some new appreciation of the variety of experiences and divine dealings with us necessary to fit us for the enjoyment of heaven. But this portion of the journey to which we have now come can be understood only by those who have suffered deeply. To most of us the sorrows and soul wrestlings here prefigured will come at some stage of our progress. To many of us they may not yet have come. Let us, however, learn the lesson of trust and obedience now, that we may not be taken unawares farther on.

The experiences of the Israelites in this portion of their journey made a deep impression upon the mind of Moses. He never forgot the valleys lying around and before Mount Hor. This was comparatively new ground to him. For forty years he had dwelt in the mountains of Midian, so that every foot of soil and rock around Dophkah and Alush and Rephidim was familiar to him; but, so far as we know, he had not been so high up in the desert of Zin. The natural scenery impressed him. The contact with the "children of Jaakan" and their evil influence upon the people under his charge depressed him. He knew how to meet Amalek, but here was a quieter, more insidious foe. What he felt and suffered in this portion of the journey is described in Deuteronomy ix. 24–29, x. 1–7. He was speaking of Hashmonah and the unbelieving numbering of the people there when he said: "Ye have been rebellious against the Lord from the day that I knew you" (Deut. ix. 24). What he did in Moseroth is described as follows: "Thus I fell down before the Lord forty days and forty nights, as I fell down at the first; because the Lord had said He would destroy you" (Deut. ix. 25). And then very clearly he describes how God led them deeper into tribulation at Bene-jaakan (Deut. x. 6), and then in the next verse tells how they came to Gudgodah, which is another form of the name which we have in Numbers xxxiii. 32, and which stands at the head of this section.

What, then, does Hor-hagidgad signify? At our last study we left the Israelites where God had been afflicting them because of their forgetfulness and sin. Indeed, for two stations we have had the subject of divine chastisement before us. Here the iron penetrates still deeper into their souls and they are made to endure still more severe afflictions. For Hor-hagidgad means "a narrow passage of great affliction." The idea seems to be taken from some narrow defile in the mountains where a pressing host might come to great disaster. The Syriac form of the word means "the eye of a needle." This is the same figure as in Matthew xix. 24. God saw best to afflict Israel here, so that they might have more and more of a desire to enter in through the "strait gate" and tread the "narrow way."

The Hebrew word from which the name of this station is taken is very expressive. It contains a suggestion of the darkness, narrowness, dismalness of a rocky defile in the mountains. How often have we felt the gloom and oppression of such a place! In 1 Samuel xiv. 11 the word is rendered "hole." In many passages it is translated "cave." David found himself in many such places in the course of his life, and so did the Covenanters, Waldensians, and other faithful children of the Lord. In 2 Kings xii. 9 the same word is used of the little hole Jehoiada bored in the lid of the chest. The thought is of narrowness, oppression, and straitening. Let us form a mental picture of the Israelites away in some dark, gloomy, dripping mountain fastness, crowded together in physical stress and misery, while the whole outward picture was painfully realized in the affliction and despair of their souls. God was dealing with them, and for the present it was not joyous, but grievous.

For us the lesson is plain. One stroke of the rod is not always sufficient to humble us. Even two strokes may not suffice, and God needs to add Hor-hagidgad to Bene-jaakan. Hard names they are to us; hard lessons they contained for Israel, and pass on to us. We do not desire to "agonize to enter in at the strait gate"; so God finds it necessary to afflict us again and again. There is a remarkable passage in Proverbs iii. 11, quoted by the writer of the Hebrews (xii. 5), that runs as follows: "My son, despise not the chastening of the Lord; neither be weary of His correction." Here we have the two extremes into which a Christian may fall. We may either despise or despond, be impatient or stolid. Both of these we are to avoid. Nor are we to oscillate to and fro as a pendulum under the trials sent upon us; for this is the meaning of 1 Thessalonians iii. 3: "That no man should be moved by these afflictions." A calm, trusting course toward the heavenly Canaan God would have us take.

An even progress in the midst of sunshine or storm is the ideal speed of a ship; the same is the ideal life of a Christian. What growth of inward mortification, what habitual self-denial, what constant renunciation of our own wills does this imply!

At this station the Israelites probably were feeling very painfully the punishment for their disobedience that God meted out to them. They had sinned in distrusting God, and therefore they were to die in the wilderness. In the dark and clammy defiles of the mountains many of the aged and more feeble ones would drop by the wayside. What a picture would have met the eyes of any traveler who followed their course over the deserts and through the mountains! Bodies were lying on every side, some of them in shallow graves, some of them thrust hastily into sepulchers hewn out of the rocks, and some bones left for the wild beasts to pick and then to whiten in the sun.

It must have been about this time that the Ninetieth Psalm was written. You will observe that this psalm was written by "Moses, the man of God." And if we think of what was going on at Hor-hagidgad, the people dying in multitudes and the iron of well-deserved affliction entering into their souls, we will understand the psalm. "Thou turnest man to destruction," it says. How vivid this must have been to the writer! "For all our days are passed away in Thy wrath." They had nothing but death to look forward to, because of disobedience. "Who knoweth the power of Thine anger?" It seemed as if God would never relent; yet through it all were tokens of mercy. "Thou sayest, Return, ye children of men. . . . Make us glad. Satisfy us early; that we may rejoice and be glad. Let the beauty of the Lord our God be upon us." In wrath God remembers mercy.

Oh, how much better is our prospect in affliction! We have heaven to look forward to as a Canaan that may be reached. We have Christ's smile lighting upon us even through the darkness. We have His words echoing in our hearts: "Let not your heart be troubled."

XXX

JOTBATHAH

EMERGING from the defile in the mountains where such sore tribulation had descended upon the Israelites, we find them coming into a wide and fertile land watered by sparkling rivers. What a refreshing change it must have been from gloom to sunshine, from distress to rest and refreshment! Moses distinctly calls the region "a land of rivers of waters" (Deut. x. 7). He calls the station at which they pitched their camp "Jotbath." This is the same as he had catalogued as "Jotbathah" in Numbers xxxiii. 33. It was a beautiful and refreshing place, to be compared with Elim, where fountains and palm groves were; and, like Elim, it follows close upon stations where punishment had been meted out to the rebellious people. In the midst of wrath God always remembers mercy. And from this we may learn that when we humble ourselves and turn completely to the Lord, He will lead us into refreshing places.

"Jotbathah" means literally "goodness." Through the great afflictions of the last three stations they had come to a place where the divine goodness was bestowed upon them. God had promised to bring Israel into a good land (Exod. iii. 8), and here He was fulfilling the promise. Doubtless the Israelites were surprised when they were brought to this station through so much suffering; but it was their own fault, and it is the same with us. If we are to enjoy the Spirit's blessing it must come through mortification of the flesh. "If we have been planted together in the likeness of His death, we shall be also in the likeness of His resurrection" (Rom. vi. 6). At Hor-hagidgad we die unto self and to the world, but we come at once to taste and to see that the Lord is "good," and we find ourselves at the station where "is a river, the streams whereof shall make glad the city of God" (Ps. xlvi. 4).

Goodness as an attribute of God needs a word of explanation. It is not to be confounded with grace or mercy or even love. Goodness, like wisdom and justice and truth, is an inherent attribute of God. They are necessary to Him, so to speak, and are not at all dependent upon an act of His will. They are like the light and warmth of the sun. As long as the sun exists it must give light and warmth. But grace and mercy are dependent upon God's will. He *wishes* to be gracious, He *chooses* to be merciful. By an exercise of His will He applies His goodness to a particular heart in a particular way at a particular time. If the heart is guilty we call this application of goodness "grace." If the heart is miserable we call it "mercy." The *g's* go together—grace, guilty; and the *m's* go together—mercy, miserable. Take an illustration. The sun must always shine, and if any plant or flower is in the range of its rays that plant or flower will grow to be beautiful. But let us suppose that there is a little violet under the edge of an overhanging rock, and the sun *wills* to bend one of its rays around the edge of the rock to touch the flower and cause it to lift up its head. That volition changes the ray of sunlight from mere goodness to grace or mercy, as the case might be.

Goodness being an inherent, essential trait of God, it is no wonder that our ancestors should choose this for the very name of Deity; for God simply means "the Good One." Paul delights to use the intensive word "riches" when speaking of the divine goodness, as in Romans ii. 4: "The riches of His goodness and forbearance and long-suffering." Wyclif translates thus, "richesses," so strong and full is the plural in the Greek. (See also Eph. i. 7, ii. 4, 7, iii. 8; Rom. ix. 23; Phil. iv. 19.)

It was probably at Jotbathah that Moses first sang the wonderful psalm given in Deuteronomy x. 12–22. How appropriate its opening stanza: "And now, Israel, what doth the Lord thy God require of thee, but to fear the Lord thy God, to walk in all His ways, and to love Him, and to serve the Lord thy God with all thy heart and with all thy soul?" (Verse 12.) The psalm deals throughout with the goodness of God, as was most fitting, since before the eyes of the author spread the goodly plain watered by the flowing rivers. What an object-lesson it was to him, particularly as he could see the tents of the resting Israelites dotting that plain! Notice seven things in this psalm:

1. *God is good* (verse 12). This is the fundamental idea, and Moses was familiar with it. He had experienced "the good will of Him that dwelt in the bush" (Deut. xxxiii. 16; Rom. xii. 2).

2. *God deviseth good things.* "To keep the commandments of the Lord, and His statutes, which I command thee this day for thy good" (verse 13). Frequently we read in the Scriptures of "the good hand of our God" (Ezra viii. 18, 22). The royal bounty of Solomon was only an example of this, for in the margin it is described as "according to the hand of King Solomon" (1 Kings x. 13).

3. *God shows His goodness by delighting in His people.* "Only the Lord had a delight in thy fathers to love them, and He chose their seed after them, even you above all people, as it is this day" (verse 15). We read much of the "pleasure" of the divine goodness. (See Eph. i. 5.) "The good pleasure of His goodness" even is spoken of—a remarkable piling up of sweet thoughts (2 Thess. i. 11). As a good person delights in benefiting others, so God delights in blessing His children.

4. *God's goodness implies greatness and judgment.* "For the Lord your God is God of gods, and Lord of lords, a great God, a mighty, and a terrible, which regardeth not persons, nor taketh reward: He doth execute the judgment of the fatherless and widow, and loveth the stranger, in giving him food and raiment" (verses 17, 18). The junction of the two thoughts is very clear in Nahum i. 6, 7. The first temptation was to cast a doubt upon the goodness of the Lord (Gen. iii. 1).

5. *God's goodness demands brotherly love.* "Love ye therefore the stranger: for ye were strangers in the land of Egypt" (verse 19). How can man possibly enjoy the goodness of the Father without reflecting it upon other lives? (1 John iv. 20.)

6. *God's goodness requires obedience.* "Thou shalt fear the Lord thy God; Him shalt thou serve, and to Him shalt thou cleave, and swear by His name" (verse 20). As naturally as the flower lifts up its head in the sunlight, so does the Christian's heart respond in gratitude to God's kind dealings. See the praise of His "good promise" in 1 Kings viii. 56. See how even repentance is based on God's goodness (Rom. ii. 4).

7. *God's goodness necessitates praise.* "He is thy praise, and He is thy God, that hath done for thee these great and terrible things, which thine eyes have seen" (verse 21). The psalmist's deepest and most worshipful theme running all through his hymns of praise is the divine goodness. (See Ps. xxv. 8, xxxiv. 8, lxxiii. 1, lxxxv. 6, c. 5, cvi. 1, cvii. 1, cviii. 1; and many other passages.)

The "good things" of God are all summarized in the Holy Spirit, who, with the blessed Redeemer, is God's best gift to man. See how this idea is brought out in Matthew vii. 11, compared with Luke xi. 13. What good thing can the Christian desire that is not comprehended in the gift of the Holy Spirit? If we realized this we would exclaim with the psalmist, "Oh how great is Thy goodness, . . . which Thou hast wrought for them that trust in Thee before the sons of men!" (Ps. xxxi. 19.) To trust God and come under the blessing of the Holy Spirit is to come into the station of "goodness" with us as well as with the psalmist (Ps. xxiii. 6).

XXXI

EBRONAH

Out of the peaceful plain watered by rivers the Israelites must take their journey, and so we read that, removing from Jotbathah, they encamped at Ebronah (Num. xxxiii. 34). In all probability this was not a long journey measured by miles, but when computed in experiences, it was a weary and significant descent. The word "Ebronah" means "wrath" or "the cloud of loud crying." Sudden and decided was the change from a station where the "goodness" of God was particularly manifested to a station where divine "wrath" called forth the "loud crying" and strong intercession of the people. What more vivid parable could there be of that "goodness of God" which "leads to repentance" than this departure of the people from the pleasant station and their coming into a place of penitential prayer?

Some scholars say that this station was at a ford where the Israelites passed through the Gulf of Ælana. We are now approaching Ezion-gaber, which was a seaport on this gulf near its head. The host under Moses may, therefore, have come to this place, where they were compelled to pass through the waters. The scene may have aroused memories of the destruction of Pharaoh and his armies. The passage may have been dangerous in itself, and God may have refused to work another miracle of deliverance for them. All this is mere conjecture founded, more or less reliably, upon the etymology of the word " Ebronah," or " Abronah," as Smith gives it in his Bible dictionary. But a reference to these suppositions of scholars may serve at least to fix a picture of the station in our minds.

The sudden transition from the light and favor of Jotbathah to the gloom and sorrow of Ebronah is very true to life—to Christian life. God in His wisdom orders these changes with three aims probably in view: (1) to develop humility in us; (2) to discover and destroy selfhood, which is very apt to increase when we are in pleasant spiritual places; (3) to teach us deep resignation and true poverty of spirit in prosperity, so that we may be blessed indeed and come to enjoy the kingdom of heaven (Matt. v. 3).

Among the many passages in which occurs the Hebrew word from which "Ebronah" comes, the following may be referred to, all containing the idea of "wrath": Genesis xlix. 7; Job xxi. 30; Psalm xc. 9; Proverbs xi. 4; Isaiah x. 6; Jeremiah vii. 29; Lamentations ii. 2; Ezekiel vii. 19; Hosea v. 10; Habakkuk iii. 8. Thirty-four times the word is used with this meaning in the Old Testament.

To be under God's "wrath" is to be under a "cloud" indeed, and hence we find the Hebrew root often used in the sense of a cloud. A very pathetic example is Lamentations ii. 1, where the weeping prophet, feeling that the people were deprived of God's favoring smile, exclaims, "How hath the Lord covered the daughter of Zion with a cloud in His anger, and cast down from heaven unto the earth the beauty of Israel, and remembered not His footstool in the day of His anger!" No wonder that under these circumstances the daughter of Zion is described as humbling herself in penitence and hanging down her head in true shame (verse 10). The same Hebrew word is used in 1 Kings xviii. 44, 45, where the cloud is described which Elijah's servant beheld from Carmel rising out of the sea, and by which the heavens were overspread with darkness and tumultuous rain.

The Ebronah state finds illustration in three main directions:

1. *In the example of our Lord.*

Have you ever stopped to consider the meaning of Hebrews v. 7? "Who in the days of His flesh, when He had offered up prayers and supplications with strong crying and tears unto Him that was able to save Him from death, and was heard in that He feared." What bitterness of soul is thus expressed! We are accustomed to think of our blessed Jesus as weeping in the garden of Gethsemane and crying out in pain and agony on the cross, but this passage represents His burden as habitual during all the days of His residence in the flesh. We read of His retiring to the top of dark mountains and spending whole nights in prayer (Luke vi. 12), and it was all to encourage us to pray, and not to faint (Luke xviii. 1). So that when Christ cried out on the cross, "My God, My God, why hast Thou forsaken Me?" He was but finishing up the misery of which His whole life, for our sakes and for the world's sake, was full. Oh, when we think of all that our Lord suffered for us, shall we not find our hearts going out to Him in love and "strong crying"?

2. *In the believer's sore stress of affliction.*

We have come upon this thought more than once, but here we meet it again. In His wisdom God causes us to be disciplined by the pressures of many sorrows until we lift up our voices as the people did at Ebronah, crying mightily unto Him who dwelt in the heavens for support and deliverance. See how it was with David: "I sink in deep mire, where there is no standing: I am come into deep waters, where the floods overflow me" (Ps. lxix. 2). See how it was with Heman the Ezrahite: "But unto Thee have I cried, O Lord; and in the morning shall my prayer prevent Thee" (Ps. lxxxviii. 13). So has it been with all of God's perfected saints from their day to ours. Read through the Twenty-second Psalm, and mark how many things mentioned in it have been true in your case already.

3. *In the believer's entering into the cloud of doubt.*

All of God's children, as of old, are "baptized in the cloud"—in *some* cloud. But there are some who "fear as they enter into the cloud" (Luke ix. 34). They are distressed by doubts or tempted to hesitate by their timid natures. I believe that God deals very tenderly with such. We are never to forget that the mere arising of a doubt in our minds is not sin. It is only when we harbor that doubt, and fondle it and follow it, that it becomes sin to us. Cherished difficulties are real difficulties. If, through a timid nature or a natural disposition to question all matters, we are approached in temptation by Satan, we are not therefore to despair. This is our Ebronah. Let us cry out unto God. If we really *want* to believe God will help us to believe. This was the attitude of the father of the demoniac child when he said, "Lord, I believe; help Thou mine unbelief" (Mark ix. 24). If we can truly say that, we need never despair.

XXXII

EZION-GABER

FROM Ebronah the Israelites, we are told, journeyed to Ezion-gaber and encamped there (Num. xxxiii. 35). We come now to familiar ground again. This station has been identified by the Sinai Exploration Expedition, and its location may be seen upon the map in your Bible. Ezion-gaber is mentioned in several passages of Scripture, and seems to have been the scene of many important transactions. It was a haven for ships on the shore of that upper arm of the Red Sea known as the Gulf of Ælana (1 Kings ix. 26). It was in the country of Edom, which land was afterward subdued by David (2 Sam. viii. 14). It was in this port that Solomon built a navy to fetch gold from Ophir (1 Kings ix. 26, 28), and to this port the navy returned once in three years with the stores of precious metal (1 Kings x. 22).

The literal meaning of the name is "the counsel of strength." The word occurs with this meaning in 2 Samuel xxii. 33: "God is my strength and power; and He maketh my way perfect." This strength of counsel is attributed to our Lord Jesus in Isaiah ix. 6, being there called El Gibar, or Gaber, "The mighty God," and the "Counselor" as well. He is said in Isaiah lxiii. 1 to be "mighty to save," and His mission as explained in Titus ii. 14 was to save from all iniquity. Drawing an illustration, therefore, from this station, as we have done from the other camping-places in the wilderness, we learn that the Christian on his way to the heavenly Canaan needs to come frequently into places where he may enjoy the strong counsel of Christ. This it is that will make us "perfect, even as our Father which is in heaven is perfect" (Matt. v. 48). This counsel is the truth by which we are to be sanctified (John xvii. 17). By it we are enabled to overcome sin, and resist the assaults of the devil, and conquer through patience and the blood of the Lamb; for "if we confess our sins, He is faithful and just to forgive us our sins, and to cleanse us from all unrighteousness" (1 John i. 9).

1. In many trying circumstances men have found "the counsel of God" a benefit and a blessing; but it must be sought humbly and with a true and faithful heart. Study carefully the import of the following passages: "And they said unto him, Ask counsel, we pray thee, of God, that we may know whether our way which we go shall be prosperous" (Judg. xviii. 5); "And the children of Israel arose, and went up to the house of God, and asked counsel of God, and said, Which of us shall go up first to the battle against the children of Benjamin? And the Lord said, Judah shall go up first" (Judg. xx. 18); "And Saul asked counsel of God, Shall I go down after the Philistines? wilt Thou deliver them into the hand of Israel? But He answered him not that day" (1 Sam. xiv. 37);

"The counsel of the Lord standeth forever, the thoughts of His heart to all generations" (Ps. xxxiii. 11); "And the land of Judah shall be a terror unto Egypt, every one that maketh mention thereof shall be afraid in himself, because of the counsel of the Lord of hosts, which He hath determined against it" (Isa. xix. 17); "For who hath stood in the counsel of the Lord, and hath perceived and heard His word? who hath marked His word, and heard it?" (Jer. xxiii. 18); "But the Pharisees and lawyers rejected the counsel of God against themselves, being not baptized of Him" (Luke vii. 30); "Him, being delivered by the determinate counsel and foreknowledge of God, ye have taken, and by wicked hands have crucified and slain" (Acts ii. 23).

What a blessing and a comfort to the Christian that he has a risen Lord to whom he can go at any moment for counsel and strength! In the darkness of night, in the hurry of business, in the suddenness of loss and calamity, in the desolation of grief, we have but to turn our hearts upward, and lo! we are at the spiritual Ezion-gaber. The Saviour's face smiles upon us, the Saviour's voice speaks peace and strength to us. Christ is appropriately called a Counselor, because of His infinite wisdom (Col. ii. 3), as well as on account of His perfect willingness to instruct us and to plead our cause before God's throne (Rev. iii. 18; 1 John ii. 1).

As to the manner in which Christ gives the Christian counsel, study the following passages: Isaiah l. 4; Matthew xi. 29; Mark iv. 33, 34; John xvi. 12. With what unwearied love did He receive all who wished to converse with Him! (See Mark ii. 13, iii. 20, 21; John

iii. 1, iv. 6.) We may go to Him with perfect confidence, knowing that He heareth us, "whatsoever we ask."

2. Besides the thought of counsel, there is in this station the blessed thought of "strength." One of the bitterest reflections to philosophers who sincerely desired the moral advancement of their fellows has been that they could tell men what to do, but could not give them the power to do it. Rome was full of wise maxims when Paul wrote his Epistle to the Romans, but the thing Paul gloried in most was that he had a gospel which was not only good counsel, but available strength —that "it is the *power* of God unto salvation to every one that believeth" (Rom. i. 16). Neither Epicurean nor Stoic had been able to promise such a thing before. They could write down a list of virtues to be copied, but they could not supply the motive and impetus to enable men to be virtuous. Here is where our blessed Lord transcends all philosophers. "All His commands are enablings." Ezion is linked to Gaber. We can "be strong in the Lord, and in the power of His might" (Eph. vi. 10). There were four different Greek words meaning "power" (*kratos, ischus, dunamis,* and *energeia,* meaning power in every essential of its nature and all forms of operation), and all of these are used by the apostle to teach how fully and blessedly our Lord will apply His strength unto us in our weakness. (See Eph. i. 19, 20.) Note that all four Greek words above indicated are brought together for emphasis in this one passage.

3. There is, however, a lesson of warning for us at our Ezion-gaber station. What detailed counsel God

gave the Israelites here we do not know, but it seems probable from Deuteronomy ii. 8, 9, that one lesson given them was, " Distress not the Moabites, neither contend with them in battle." They were not to go out in their own strength. They were to wait upon God's order to march against the enemy. So the Christian needs to learn the lesson of patient waiting. In our zeal we may outrun the Lord. If the counsel of Jesus is followed it becomes to us the means of life and peace. If it be not followed it is a rock of destruction to us.

As the Israelites stood on the shore of the sea that day, and looked at the waves breaking over the rocks, a particular ledge being called "the Giant's Backbone," they must have received an impression of the lurking of danger at the very mouth of that harbor. They could not know that the ships of Jehoshaphat would afterward be "broken" upon those very rocks (1 Kings xxii. 48), but they could see danger-signals flying in the spray. Ezion-gaber might have taught them that going in the same boat with evil men is bad and dangerous business (2 Chron. xx. 36). Oh, that we might take warning in view of the "counsel" given us, the knowledge and privileges afforded us! If we improve all these aright they shall be a "savor of life unto life" to us; if not, a "savor of death unto death." If any man instructed in the truth fall upon the rock, he shall be broken as the ships of Jehoshaphat were. If that rock fall in sovereign wrath and strength upon any man, he shall be ground to powder.

XXXIII

KADESH

I HAVE already indicated the explanation I prefer of the apparent confusion about this word "Kadesh." It represents a region rather than a station, a whole locality, or, as we would say, a "county," in the upper desert. With this agrees the verse in Numbers to which we have now come: "And they removed from Eziongaber, and pitched in the wilderness of Zin, which is Kadesh" (Num. xxxiii. 36). To some spot in this general region the Israelites formerly came, and it was there that the timorous report of the spies was returned to the people. Since then they had been marching hither and thither in perplexity and distress, their carcasses falling by the wayside.

Now they come back to the region and establish a camp, possibly at the point indicated on the map as Kadesh-barnea. A number of very important events transpired here, and it will therefore be convenient to divide our study into two parts.

First let us take up the phrase, "wilderness of Zin" or "Tzin," and study its significance both physical and spiritual. The word "Zin" or "Tzin" means "a sharp dart," "coldness," "a shield." There is some confusion here, but we may leave scholars to settle the etymological questions and relations. It may have been that it was a region of thorns and briers, which are very often found in such deserts; or the name may have come from the coolness of the refreshing waters God caused to flow there for the people. We need not delay upon the physical features; the spiritual lessons are apparent and important.

It was evidently a place of sharp trials and temptations—so sharp as rightly to be compared with thorns or darts. The word from which Zin comes is used metaphorically in the fifty-fifth verse of the thirty-third chapter of Numbers, as follows: "But if ye will not drive out the inhabitants of the land from before you; then it shall come to pass, that those which ye let remain of them shall be pricks in your eyes, and thorns in your sides, and shall vex you in the land wherein ye dwell." A similar use of the word we have in Proverbs xxii. 5: "Thorns and snares are in the way of the froward: he that doth keep his soul shall be far from them." (See also Josh. xxiii. 13.) So that we are authorized to notice a comparison between the thorns which grew in the desert and pierced the bodies of the people and the inward trials which rent their souls.

Turning to the twentieth chapter of Numbers, we find a very thrilling story of what occurred at this station. Notice:

1. Here Miriam died (verse 1), and here was she buried. What simple record the Bible gives of the death and burial of even the leaders of God's host of saints in all ages! In God's eyes the life is everything

and the death nothing. If life be conducted upon principles of truth and righteousness, the death is simply the opening of a door to admit to God's presence. A great many verses are concerned with Miriam's life, but a single line describes her death. Thirteen chapters and seven verses are given to Abraham's life, but his death is recorded in a single verse. Joseph's experiences and exploits form the theme of fourteen chapters, but the death of Egypt's great prime minister is described in three lines. David appears in nearly every chapter of 1 and 2 Samuel, the first two chapters of 1 Kings, and a part of 1 Chronicles, yet the great king and psalmist goes off the stage in this simple statement: "So David slept with his fathers, and was buried in the city of David." Paul's conversion and ministry concerns the whole Book of Acts from the ninth chapter onward, yet the death of the great apostle to the Gentiles is not considered of enough importance even to record. Miriam was a prophetess and was reckoned by the Lord as one of the chief leaders of Israel (Micah vi. 4), yet how wondrously simple is the announcement of her death!

2. Scarcity of water again afflicts the people. This difficulty was common in the desert, but here it seems to have been particularly distressing (verses 2, 4), involving the cattle as well as the people in suffering. So the Israelites are led to say complainingly (verse 5), "Wherefore have ye made us to come up out of Egypt, to bring us in unto this evil place? It is no place of seed, or of figs, or of vines, or of pomegranates; neither is there any water to drink." In the Vulgate and Chaldee versions this expression "evil place" is rendered, "this

worst place." It seems to have been the worst situation, in their judgment, into which they had been brought.

3. A third occurrence at this station was the giving of the miraculous supply of water from the rock (verses 8–11), and the consequent announcement of God that neither Moses nor Aaron, because of their unbelief, should go personally into the Promised Land. All that we need to know about the sin of Moses, which is so puzzling to many Bible students, is given in the twelfth verse: "And the Lord spake unto Moses and Aaron, Because ye believed Me not, to sanctify Me in the eyes of the children of Israel, therefore ye shall not bring this congregation into the land which I have given them." What a sharp thorn this must have been to the two men who had so long led the people! Truly it was the "wilderness of Zin" to them. Let us beware lest we fall after the same example of unbelief.

4. The people gathered themselves together against Moses and murmured on account of their thirst. This is a fourth thing to be noted at this station. Satan wounded them by piercing them through and through with the thorn of discontent. Their obedience was weakened. They grieved the good Spirit of God. They came into that rebellious state to which Satan so loves to lead the child of God, and which may very appropriately be called "the wilderness of thorns." The result was that God gave them over to their enemies. Edom raised an insolent cry against them, and God refused to interfere. In disgrace and humiliation Israel was compelled to "turn away" from the borders of Edom (verses 14–21). What a humiliating picture of defeat suffered by the Christian who has been weak-

ened by unbelief and is resisting the sweet power of the Holy Ghost in the heart!

5. But the word "Zin" or "Tzin" also signifies "cold" or "coolness," and in this we have a beautiful spiritual lesson. The hot sun of the desert was shedding its piercing rays upon Israel from above, and the darts of discontent were piercing the hearts of the people within; yet God sent them coolness and refreshment in the waters that flowed from the rock. Oh, the wonderful mercy of our God! The word from which Zin comes is used in Proverbs xxv. 13 : "As the cold of snow in the time of harvest, so is a faithful messenger to them that send him: for he refresheth the soul of his masters." God Himself was the faithful messenger to Israel at Kadesh, refreshing their souls with counsel and peace as grateful as "the cold of snow in the time of harvest."

6. The last meaning of "Zin," as given above, is "a shield." The sequence of ideas is not difficult to discover. As the refreshing waters from the rock proved a defense or shield to the Israelites from the scorching rays of the sun, so the shield of faith quenches the fiery darts of the devil for us. Bromley and other scholars think that the apostle's very unusual figure of speech in Ephesians vi. 16 is drawn from the conjunction of ideas here hinted at. The Hebrew *tzinnah*, or "shield," took its name from *tzanan*, "to cool." Paul therefore refers to the inflaming of the blood and spirits by the darts of the adversary, and the quenching of them through an exercise of faith. It is certainly an important lesson for us to learn, at whatever stage of our wilderness journey we may have arrived.

XXXIV

KADESH (*Continued*).

WE have so far considered at this station the word "Tzin" or "Zin." The lessons which we have found have concerned the hardships and trials of our desert experience. In the word "Kadesh" we come to pleasanter thoughts. The word signifies "sanctification" or "holiness." All through the desert wanderings God has had in view the sanctification of His people. All through our earthly pilgrimage the loving Father is yearning to bring us to holiness. Notice:

1. *The reason for giving this name to the station.*

In the twentieth chapter of Numbers, at the thirteenth verse, it is stated that the place was called "Kadesh" because the Israelites there "strove with the Lord, and He was sanctified in them." That is to say, He showed Himself holy, vindicated His attributes, and justified all His course with them by giving the miraculous outpouring of water. We might with profit observe how many of God's attributes are vindicated in this scene. His power appears in the working of so great and sudden a miracle, His mercy in pardoning their murmurings and subduing their inclinations to rebellion, His great goodness and bounty in affording such abundance of water when the drought was so great and their necessities so pressing. His truth appears in preserving them alive, notwithstanding their sins and complaints, in order that His promise of bringing them to the good land might be kept. His justice is shown in His severity toward Moses and Aaron in solemnly protesting that they should not lead the people into the Promised Land (verse 20). "It went ill with Moses for their sakes" (Ps. cvi. 32). These and other attributes of God shine forth very clearly in this transaction, and hence it is said that He sanctified Himself there.

2. *The identity between the wilderness of Zin and Kadesh.*

"They pitched in the wilderness of Zin, *which is* Kadesh." The one locality is merged in the other. Doubtless Kadesh was a section of the larger wilderness of Zin; but spiritually it is very significant that the place of thorns and trials should be identified with the work of sanctification. We must be made perfect through suffering, as our Saviour was. To our day and throughout all time the station of holiness lies in the desert of the fiery thorns. Does not this remind us of 2 Corinthians xii. 7, where Paul's thorn in the flesh is described as leading him to sanctification? Indeed, it is a great lesson for us to learn that under the fiery darts of the devil (Eph. vi. 16) we are really in the position of the Israelites at Kadesh. God would have us learn resignation, He would have us merge our wills in His, that we may escape the Israelites' sin and rebellious murmurings, which were written down for our instruction, that we should not lust and murmur, as they did (1 Cor. x. 6), nor "think it strange concerning the fiery trial which is to try us" (1 Pet. iv. 12).

3. *The work of sanctification itself is a work of cleansing.*

How sweetly are we here taught that God has abundant waters for us and that He has promised to pour them forth! "I will pour water upon him that is thirsty, and floods upon the dry ground: I will pour My Spirit upon thy seed, and My blessing upon thine offspring" (Isa. xliv. 3). This divine river is ever flowing to quench our thirst, to cool our internal fevers, to nourish our faith in God, and give us new views of His mercy, "which endureth forever." Thus God becomes sanctified in us and we are sanctified in Him. This river flows on forever, and so does the work of sanctification progress so long as our need shall be. Justification is an act of God's free grace, but sanctification is a work of God's free Spirit. We are not to content ourselves with a partial or a tardy work of cleansing. The river of divine grace runs brimming ever to the full, and we are to drink and live. Our sanctification may progress upon the low levels or the high planes, just as we choose. Full surrender to the Spirit of God, deep indrinking of this water of grace, result in high and blessed attainments.

4. *The result of this work is holiness.*

Here at Kadesh God clearly revealed that the law can make nothing perfect. Moses and Aaron were pronounced unfit to lead the people in. A better leader was provided in Joshua. And this Joshua prefigured Jesus, the great minister of love, "who gave

Himself for us, that He might redeem us from all iniquity" (Tit. ii. 14). Holiness simply means wholeness, health, completeness. To this Jesus alone can lead us by His Spirit. Holiness thus becomes the most practical, as it is the most blessed, of matters. (See St. Paul's three rules for a holy life as given in 1 Cor. x. 31; Col. iii. 17, 23.) The saints of God—that is to say, the sanctified ones of God—will therefore not be afraid of the word "holiness." It means that wholehearted life of trust and service to which our Joshua, through the power and indwelling of the blessed Spirit, is only too glad to lead us.

It will be remembered that when we were studying the experiences of Israel at Rephidim we found much that is the same in that station and in this. There were the same murmurings, the same trials and punishments, and a similar pouring forth of water out of the rock. It may be asked if there be any difference between this station and that. Notice that the subjects of temptation in Rephidim were the fathers of the people who are tested at Kadesh. Most of those fathers were now dead, as God had threatened (Deut. ii. 14), so that Kadesh implies the soul under a new dispensation, at a point of greater progress and fuller surrender to the Spirit.

Kadesh indicates also that deeper and more severe testing which comes to the advanced Christian. And it will be noticed that Israel at Kadesh endured the trials to better purpose. They are led on to greater sanctification. The dispensation of sorrow produced in them the peaceable fruit of righteousness. They humbled themselves under the mighty hand of God with more trustfulness and alacrity, and thus were led sooner out into the plains to "rest under the palm-trees" (Deut. xxxiv. 3). So is it always with advanced Christians. Trials come to them as to others, trials possibly deeper, more subtle, more distressing; but they know better how to endure them; they count it "joy" that they have fallen into them; they are more willing to "let patience have her perfect work, that they may be perfect and entire, wanting nothing" (James i. 4). Hence Kadesh is a great advance upon Etham, which we have already studied. The "perfection" of the Etham stage means consecration, entire devotedness to the Lord through the Spirit. The "holiness" of the Kadesh stage implies a progress in subjective sanctification. The heart has become purer, the desires higher. We are altogether nearer the standard of "faultlessness" than we could be at the entering into the desert. At the very first we may be "blameless"; at the last we shall be "faultless." Kadesh indicates a long step toward the latter. Let us thank God for sanctification as heartily as for justification.

XXXV

MOUNT HOR

WE are now coming upon very interesting ground. The wanderings of the Israelites in the desert are drawing to a close, and one and another of the prominent personages are passing off the scene. Miriam had died at Kadesh. Her work and testimony were ended. Others are to follow her in rapid succession. The workers fall, but the work goes on. Let this be one of the lessons we learn as we follow the Israelitish host winding up from the low valleys to the heights of Mount Hor. Clearer and wider views have now to come before our vision, even as to the people there came wider prospects of Moab and Edom. Let us notice:

1. *The death of Aaron.*

At the command of God, Aaron takes his way to the topmost rocks of Mount Hor, and there dies in the hundred and twenty-third year of his age and the fortieth from their coming out of Egypt (Num. xx. 23–29). How many of the sons of God die upon the mountain-tops! May it thus be spiritually with us. It was upon the first day of the fifth month, about the middle of our July, that Aaron, who had so long borne the burdens of the priesthood, ascended up to be divested of his robes and of his bodily tabernacle at the command of God. His work was done, and its successes and failures are alike hidden within the peaceful habitations into which God took him.

2. *The investiture of Eleazar.*

At the command of God, Moses stripped Aaron of his garments and put them upon Eleazar, his son (Num. xx. 28). In this we see a significant representation of the passing away of the Levitical priesthood, "for the wickedness and unprofitableness thereof" (Heb. vii. 18).

The very name of the successor of Aaron favors this interpretation, for "Eleazar" means "the help of God." How strongly does this bring to mind such passages as the following, in which our Lord is described: "I have laid help upon one that is mighty" (Ps. lxxxix. 19); "Mighty to save" (Isa. lxiii. 1); "A horn of salvation to save us from our enemies, and from the hand of all that hate us" (Luke i. 69, 71). Our blessed Lord is the tender and sufficient High Priest who stepped in to save when the law had failed.

3. *The great mystery of Christ in us.*

The literal meaning of the word "Hor" is "conception" or "travail," and should be taken to prefigure the forming of Christ and the Christly nature within us. Paul seems to refer to it when he says in Galatians iv. 19, "My little children, of whom I travail in birth again until Christ be formed in you." What a sacred suggestion! The specific thing the apostle desired was that Christ might fully be formed in the hearts of those Galatian believers even as the babe is in the mother's womb. When the Christian truly comes to this blessed mount that experience becomes his: Christ is formed within as "the hope of glory" (Col. i. 27). At the moment of regeneration this blessed life begins in us, but the full realization of its power may not come to us until late in life. It depends upon our yielding to the sway of the inborn Christ more and more. Before the end of the journey, with all true Christians, the delightful experience of Mount Hor will be realized. They may be more or less subject to bondage through the fear of death all their lives, but the light and peace of the mount will come at length. Dying grace will be given before the dying hour; like Aaron, they will feel themselves gently laid away by the hands of a loving God.

4. *Still further opposition encountered.*

There is one other lesson to be learned at this station. Even down to the end of our earthly pilgrimage we must expect to meet with opposition. As soon as Eleazar was invested with priestly robes a certain king, Arad by name, a Canaanite, came out against Israel. A battle ensued, and some of the Israelites were taken prisoners (Num. xxi. 1). Now "Arad" means "a dragon," so he becomes to us a type of that old serpent who immediately attacks the Christian when some special favor has been granted. Study very carefully in this connection the twelfth chapter of the Book of Revelation. It seems as if the wonderful sign in heaven of the woman clothed with the sun, watched so maliciously by the great red dragon, were a divine commentary upon this scene upon Mount Hor. But though the dragon watches, the beloved man-child is brought forth and is caught away in safety to the heavens.

Though Arad fights and takes some prisoners, he shall not finally prevail. Israel conquered him by making a vow and through prayer unto the Lord. So may we conquer in the name of our God. At length we shall tread Satan under our feet (Rom. xvi. 20) and pursue him even to Hormah, to "utter destruction" (Num. xxi. 3, marg.). Then with what glad praise will we sing to our Eleazar, the "Lord our strength" and righteousness! Victory! What a glorious thought to the Christian! Study the suggestions of it in the palm branches (Rev. vii. 9), the thrones (Matt. xix. 28; Rev. xx. 4), the riding in triumph, scattering incense and gifts, as the Roman conquerors used to do (2 Cor. ii. 14). (See also Josh. x. 24; Mal. iv. 3; Micah vii. 10; Zech. x. 5; Ps. xlvii. 3; Rom. viii. 37.) With these blessed assurances of victory ringing in our ears we have nothing to fear.

XXXVI

ZALMONAH

It must have been with sinking hearts that the Israelites left the cool heights and wide views of Mount Hor to pitch their tents in Zalmonah (Num. xxxiii. 41). If they could have foreseen the terrible events which were to happen at this station they would have been more reluctant still to take the journey. What transpired in this low-lying valley encampment is recorded in the twenty-first chapter of Numbers and is well known to every Bible student. The account of the Israelites' experiences here struck the fancy of our blessed Lord in His boyhood, as we know from the third chapter of John. The whole scene must have flashed before His mind when talking to Nicodemus, for He said, "As Moses lifted up the serpent in the wilderness, even so must the Son of man be lifted up" (John iii. 14). And with what exaltation of love and satisfaction was He able to continue, "that whosoever believeth in Him should not perish, but have eternal life"! Notice:

1. *The giving of the name.*

It was at Zalmonah that the brazen serpent was erected for the curing of those Israelites who had been bitten by the fiery serpents sent among them because of their murmurings. Observe that at this time they were compassing the land of Edom. They were not permitted to pass through this land or to enjoy its conveniences, and yet their hearts yearned for what Edom had to offer. They fell to grumbling because of the difficulty of the way and because of the lack of bread and water. How very like they were to those Christians who skirt the pleasant pastures of the world and look enviously upon the delights which they may not share! On account of these murmurings the fiery serpents were sent, and then, at the divine command, the brazen image was erected. Hence the naming of the place. "Zalmonah" means "an image" or "the place of an image." The root from which this name comes is *tzelem*, and is used in Daniel ii. 31 of the image which Nebuchadnezzar saw in his sleep, and in Daniel iii. 1 it is applied to the image of gold which the same great king erected in the plain of Dura.

2. *The character of the scourge.*

In the Hebrew these serpents are called *seraphim*, which means "burners" (verse 6). Some suppose that they were fallen angels entering into, and for the time possessing, the serpents of the wilderness, and thus used of God for the punishment of the people. Certain it is that God did so use evil angels against Egypt. (See Ps. lxxviii. 49.) No view must be taken, however, that will at all lessen the historic authority of the record. The serpents may be called *seraphim*, or "burners," merely on account of the fiery pain of their bites, or they may be so named because they are types of the feverish temptations that had entered into the hearts of the people.

3. *The deliverance provided.*

When the people had been bitten very sore and many had died, the brazen serpent was erected on a pole, and whosoever looked to it was cured. In the Hebrew the word for serpent is *sâraph* (the singular for *serâphim*), in order to show the likeness and harmony between the cause and the cure. Observe that there was nothing in this image itself to effect a cure. On the contrary, brass would naturally make such bites worse and more painful, as Grotius and some others of the older commentators declare. Thus does God select and sanctify the most unusual means for the working of benefits. He uses salt, which of itself would cause barrenness of soil, to make fruitful fields (2 Kings ii. 21). All this tells us of the Redeemer, who gave little outward appearance of being the Saviour of the world (see 1 Cor. i. 23, 24), and who is the curer of all spiritual diseases when lifted up on the cross.

4. *The condition of the cure.*

The simple condition of receiving the cure was a look of repentant faith. It is the same that is required of the sinner who would be saved from sin (Zech. xii. 10; John v. 24).

Notice the following points of instruction:

1. The image had only the form of the reptile; there was no actual poison in it. So Christ "came in the likeness of sinful flesh" (Rom. viii. 3), though there was no sin in Him.

2. The lowliness of Christ is shown us in the choice of brass, a baser metal than silver or gold, and so more fitly represents Him who took on Him the form of a servant.

3. The great reproach which fell upon Christ is shown in the image, for He was called as bad as a serpent, and it was charged against Him that He was linked with that old serpent, the devil, in the working of miracles (Matt. xii. 24). All this fulfils Psalm xxii. 6.

4. The wisdom of Christ is shown in the figure of the serpent. (See Matt. x. 16; Isa. lii. 13; Col. ii. 15.)

5. The strength of Christ is shown in the brass of which the image was composed. (See Job xl. 18.) Oh, how we should love Him, since He is able and willing to save unto the uttermost all that come unto God by Him! Look and live, dear impenitent brother! Look and gain strength, dear Christian!

XXXVII

PUNON

THE Israelites were now skirting the Mount Seir range of commanding peaks, in the land of Edom. You will see by the map that this range runs almost due north from the head of the Gulf of Ælana. Punon you will see marked on the map as lying at the foot of the range, half-way between Zalmonah and Oboth. This station is mentioned in secular history and identified by Eusebius and Jerome and by modern travelers. It is only a short distance from Zalmonah, our last station, and it is supposed that Moses obtained from mines near Punon the metal out of which to construct the brazen serpent. At all events, there were celebrated copper-mines in the vicinity, and it is significant that one of them was located at a place called Phæno, identified by scholars with this station at which we have now arrived. It was evidently a place of some importance when the Israelites visited it, though we have no lengthy description of what transpired there. The tents of Israel were pitched in huge crescents upon the plain, and must have presented a picturesque appearance, the whole scene backed by the tall, rugged peaks of the Seir range, in whose sides the openings of the mines were clearly visible.

It is a supposition of the best scholars that the incident of the brazen serpent includes this station as well as the last. The people moved on from Zalmonah, many of them still suffering from the bites of the fiery serpents. It was necessary, therefore, for Moses to erect the healing image at Punon also, in order that those who had not previously been cured might enjoy its miraculous benefits.

Bearing this in mind, we see certain very interesting spiritual lessons in the name of the place itself and in the events which we may fairly suppose to have transpired there.

Two meanings have been attached to the word "Punon," depending upon the Hebrew root from which the name is taken. As the evidence seems to be about equally divided, they may both be mentioned and certain lessons be drawn from them.

1. *The first meaning is "great doubting," "amazement," or "distraction of mind."*

The word is so translated in Psalm lxxxviii. 15: "I am afflicted and ready to die from my youth up: while I suffer Thy terrors I am distracted." The word here translated "distracted" is that from which "Punon" comes. Rightly may this convey to our minds an impression of the great trembling and despair into which the people were thrown by the bites of the serpents. We also learn how Satan presses on from one point to another in his pursuit of us. We are not through with temptation and suffering when we have left Zalmonah. They pursue us even to Punon. This interpretation also shows us the relentless vigor with which Satan attacks us when we, like the Israelites, are near the end of our wilderness wanderings. When Canaan is just in view sore trial is apt to assail us, possibly more apt than at any other time. Gideon's band, though faint, was compelled to pursue "even to Jordan" (Judg. viii. 4), and so must we. At the last moment of life the old dragon may exert all his power to sweep us as stars out of the sky (Rev. xii. 4). The sifting process is apt to become more and more severe as we progress in sanctification (Luke xxii. 31).

It is supposed that Solomon wrote the Eighty-eighth Psalm very late in life, and that he described the struggles of the aged at the seventh verse: "Thy wrath lieth hard upon me, and Thou hast afflicted me with all Thy waves." And St. Peter comes very close to the thought of this station when he says, "Beloved, think it not strange concerning the fiery trial," or, as the Greek has it, "Be not surprised concerning the burning within you" (1 Pet. iv. 12). This is an exact description of what the heart feels when at the spiritual Punon—the fiery dragon producing many inward burnings, much doubting and consternation, and not a little fear of death. St. Paul knew what this station means, for he asserts, "We were pressed out of measure, above strength, insomuch that we despaired even of life."

How many pious saints of God have come to this pressing state of tribulation, this extremity of affliction in body and soul! Well for them if they are able, with St. Paul, to recognize the design of Providence in it: "We had the sentence of death in ourselves, that we should not trust in ourselves, but in God who raiseth the dead" (2 Cor. i. 8, 9).

There is something peculiarly touching in the doubts

which arise in the minds of the aged. The questionings of the young result from inexperience, intellectual pride, desire for the things of the world, and many other unworthy causes; but the doubts of the old come from weakness of the flesh, the worn-out heart, the weary brain, and the exhausted sympathies of those who have about completed the service which Christ has demanded of them. This makes the Punon state very pathetic. In nothing does Satan show himself so crafty and merciless an accuser as in thus attacking the trembling saints of God. But he shall not prevail against them. For a time he may cause "amazement and distraction of mind," but the end shall be peace.

2. *This brings us to the second meaning of the word "Punon," which is, "the face of the Son," "the looking on or beholding of the Son."*

How beautifully does this foreshadow the lifting up of the Son of man upon the cross, that the whole world may look to Him and live! How often in despair and distraction the weary heart has turned toward that face, which, like the face of David, is "goodly to look to"! If the aged saints to whom we refer but have faith to lift up their eyes unto Him, immediately the devil will flee from them, and angels will come to minister in peace and blessing.

This signification of "Punon" seems very striking, since it is to the Son of God we look when despairing of any other assistance. Possibly Jesus may have had something of this in His mind when He referred to the uplifted serpent as a type of Himself. Certain it is that the comparison is divinely apt and beautiful. As the devil has the power to work in the heart and fill it with burning bitterness at Punon, so Christ exerts His cooling and healing power therein also. The venom of the serpent within is counteracted by a simple look to the uplifted serpent without. Christ will transform our vile body, that it may be fashioned like unto His glorious body, "according to the inworking whereby He is able even to subdue all things unto Himself" (Phil. iii. 21, Gk.). Has He not said, "I will never leave thee, nor forsake thee" (Heb. xiii. 5), and does He not mean by this that He will take up His abode in our hearts? (John xiv. 23.) Is it not stated that there is no other name under heaven given "in men" (*en anthropois*, "in the 'uplookers'")? (Acts iv. 12.) It is on this account that Paul says he is willing to endure so much that the power of Christ may rest upon him (2 Cor. xii. 9).

"Looking unto Jesus" is therefore our attitude. We who believe in His name and are filled with the blessed hope of His appearing are the true *anthropoi* ("uplookers"). Every relation which He sustains to us contains a suggestion of our duty to be uplooking to Him. Is He our Guide? Then should we fix our eyes upon Him, that we stray not from the way. Is He our Master? The scholars turn their faces toward their Teacher to hear His words. Is He our King? The courtiers of the King face the throne. Is He our Shepherd? The sheep hear His voice and look up meekly to be blessed by His smile. Look into His kindly face and follow whithersoever He leads.

Let us not fear the desert, then, brethren, for we may always look up and see Christ's face above us; and if we fully surrender our wills to His we may feel His power always operating in our hearts.

The object of leading Israel through the desert was "to humble them, and prove them, and do them good at their latter end" (Deut. viii. 16). This reminds us of Psalm xxxvii. 37: "Mark the perfect man, and behold the upright: for the end of that man is peace." God is leading us to a glorious reward; but before the day of liberation comes we must pass through Zalmonah and Punon. Oh, but the joy will be worth all the pain, and the light of Canaan will dispel the last remembrance of the darkness of the wilderness, and the peace of Immanuel will allay all the fiery pangs of serpent bites!

XXXVIII

OBOTH

You will observe this station, on the map in your Bible, situated at the upper extremity of the Seir range of mountains. The station stands at the point where the road bends down from the high levels into the fertile plains leading on toward Bozrah and the land of Moab. A beautiful spot, yet linked with a most plain and startling warning. We have not yet reached the plains of Moab, where Balak stirred up Balaam, that great sorcerer, to curse—thus hoping to destroy—Israel. What transpired at Oboth we have no means of knowing. But the signification of the word itself seems to imply a work of preparation to resist the evil which Balaam afterward undertook to accomplish; for "Oboth" means "free" or "familiar spirits," and is so translated in Leviticus xix. 31: "Regard not them that have familiar spirits, neither seek after wizards, to be defiled by them: I am the Lord your God." The same word we have in Leviticus xx. 6, 27, and in 1 Samuel xxviii. 3, 7, 8. In this latter passage we have the well-known account of the witch of Endor, who was possessed by a familiar or evil spirit. Other passages in which the word occurs are: Deuteronomy

xviii. 11; 2 Kings xxi. 6, xxiii. 24; 1 Chronicles x. 13; 2 Chronicles xxxiii. 6; Isaiah viii. 19, xix. 3, xxix. 4. It will thus be seen how important the word is in the ethics of Holy Scripture.

1. This station of Oboth may signify simply *a state of temptation*, when God's people are tested by the solicitations of evil spirits or angels. In those days, as in our own, people were inclined to resort to sorcery in order to know the events of the future. This was one of Saul's great sins for which the Lord cut him off (1 Chron. x. 13). The temptation to rely upon such sorcery is often used in the Bible as typical of the general tendency of the natural heart to distrust God. (See Jer. xxvii. 9; Isa. xlvii. 12; Mal. iii. 5; Acts viii. 9, 11, xiii. 6, 8; Rev. ix. 21, xviii. 23, xxi. 8, xxii. 15.)

2. At Oboth the people may have had *subtler temptations* than these. There are strange hints in Scripture of the ability of evil spirits to present themselves to the minds even of true Christians. We are not to "believe every spirit, but try the spirits whether they are of God" (1 John iv. 1). We are to pray against them; we are to labor to overthrow them; we are firmly to adhere to God's will; and especially we are to search the Scriptures in order to be freed from the influences they are permitted to exert. It is supposed by many that the Saviour's promise that the Holy Ghost should reveal the "things to come," or the "things coming" (John xvi. 13), is, in part at least, to offset the tendency of the human heart to inquire improperly about the future.

It is impossible for us, in this stage of our knowledge, to settle the question as to how far evil spirits have power over us. Undoubtedly a large field of investigation is opening to the science of the times along the lines of hypnotism, spiritualism, so-called clairvoyant powers, and all phenomena of that nature. The Bible seems to point out that there is a threefold enchantment under which human beings may fall.

(*a*) The first is intellectual. St. Paul inquires of the Galatians (iii. 1), " Who hath bewitched you, that ye should not obey the truth?" Satan had leavened their minds with erroneous principles concerning the necessity of circumcision and observing the ceremonial law, even though they had believed and had received the Spirit. (See verse 2.) It was necessary that St. Paul should teach them that in Christ Jesus "neither circumcision availeth anything, nor uncircumcision, but a new creature" (Gal. vi. 15). We read of "doctrines of devils" (1 Tim. iv. 1), and St. Paul seems to be referring to these doctrines when he says, "Beware lest any man spoil you through philosophy and vain deceit" (Col. ii. 8). So that in general we may conclude that much of the skepticism of the day may properly be referred to the influence of evil spirits over the minds of men.

(*b*) The second sort of enchantment may be called moral, leading men to act wickedly under pretense of knowledge and religion. This we find referred to in the Epistle of Jude and the second chapter of 2 Peter. The results are all manner of uncleanness, covetousness, hypocrisy, injustice, despising governments, turning against the whole Christian life and all morality. All these things are mentioned and described by St. Peter in this second chapter of his second letter. St. Paul also touches upon these matters in more places than one; as, for example, 1 Timothy i. 5, 6; Ephesians vi. 12. Whatever all this may mean, at least this much is clear, that they "*wrestled* against principalities and powers, against the rulers of the darkness of this world." How much do we need to open our hearts to the true Spirit, and to be thoroughly conversant with the Word of God, in order that all evil powers and rulers of darkness may be instantly detected and summarily expelled from the temple of the heart!

(*c*) There is a third kind of influence exerted by evil spirits upon us, which may be called sensitive. There are hints in God's Word that Satan and his angels have power to produce painful disturbances in the soul, to harass us by those doubts and perturbations about which we were speaking at the last station. Job charges the evil one with "scaring him with dreams, and terrifying him through visions" (vii. 14). So dire was the distress caused his sensitive nature that he goes on to say that his soul was led to "choose strangling, and death rather than life."

Evil angels are said to be "tormentors of men," even as the holy angels are declared to be "ministering servants of men" (Heb. i. 14). We can touch only the outermost rim of this mysterious subject as yet, but this much is clear, that we need to come to that nearness with God of which we read in Numbers xxiii. 23: "Surely there is no enchantment against Jacob, neither is there any divination against Israel." In such nearness neither Satan nor his angels can exert the least power upon us otherwise than that which God allows for our good.

In this connection study carefully the twelfth chapter

of the Book of Revelation, where we have a full portrait given of our great enemy, Satan. He is shown to be a devourer (verse 4), a deceiver (verse 9), an accuser (verse 10), a persecutor (verse 13), and a blasphemer (xiii. 5, 6). Israel at Oboth may have felt the power of his malice in ways that we know not of; but such hints as we have of his bitter persecutions are matched in our experience. More than once do we pass through this trying station on our way to the heavenly Canaan. But let us not shrink or be dismayed. Our Michael still fights for us (Rev. xii. 7); we may still "overcome by the blood of the Lamb" (Rev. xii. 11). Let us comfort our hearts with the blessed assurance that all things *do* "work together for good to them that love God, to them who are the called according to His purpose" (Rom. viii. 28).

A beautiful contrast may be noted between the "familiar spirit," in whose society there is strife and dismay, and the "familiar friend," in whose society there is peace (Ps. xli. 9, marg.). The word from which this latter expression is drawn is *shalom* ("peace"). Let us take Jesus to be our "familiar Friend," the "Man of our peace," and then we shall not at all fear what the mysterious spirits of earth and air and hell can do. Let us cling to Jesus, and then we shall not be led away into extravagance by any of the fascinating theories of the times.

XXXIX

IJE-ABARIM

It must have been with great pleasure that the Israelites departed from Oboth and pursued their way straight northward across the plains to this station. In the forty-fourth verse of the thirty-third chapter of Numbers it is stated that Ije-abarim was in the border of Moab. This gives us its location and has enabled modern explorers to identify the station. On the map you will observe that it is just south of Bozrah. It is probable that the people remained here for some time, as by the spot runs the wady Zared, that is to say, " the turn of the willows," probably one of the streams which run into the southern angle of the Dead Sea. There being plenty of water here, the weary host would be allured to a longer rest than usual. What transpired at this station is not fully known; but judging from the meaning of the name, we are led to conclude that the deep work at Oboth found here its natural result. In the margin of the Bible " Ije-abarim " is said to mean " heaps of Abarim." This does not give us any great light. If we may believe Bromley and other scholars, the better meaning is " heaps of fords," or " confusion of fords." It is probable that at this point more or less confusion occurred in crossing the stream referred to above, or in deciding upon the best way to be pursued in their future journey. And it may be that discussions arose among the people because some of them had been led into fanaticism by the sorcerers and necromancers consulted at Oboth. Spiritually we may take the station to indicate that confusion of mind and uncertainty of judgment in the pilgrims toward heaven when temporarily they do not see clearly their way. It may be that for wise purposes the divine light is withdrawn, or that a cloud is allowed to intervene, or that fresh and great trials and temptations are permitted to fall. The pilgrim, therefore, is in the position of a traveler in a desert when he comes to a confused variety of ways or paths crossing one another, and knows not which to take; or to a river that has many fords, some safe, but most of them dangerous, and, to make matters worse, such guides as offer themselves contradicting one another. Jacob was in such a strait (Gen. xxxii.) when he heard that Esau was coming against him with four hundred men; Israel was in such a strait at the Red Sea, and so was Abraham when he was learning to believe in hope against hope. St. Paul was in such a strait when he was being taught not to trust in himself, but in God, who raiseth the dead (2 Cor. i. 9).

There are plenty of over-zealous leaders who in this age of the world are calling "Lo here!" and "Lo there!" Indeed, the church has always needed to guard herself against the vehemence of false zeal. In our Saviour's day the scribes and Pharisees were eager to compass sea and land to make a proselyte, but the result was that he became twofold more corrupt than themselves (Matt. xxiii. 15). True zeal exercises itself in laboring to draw one and another from darkness to light, from the power of Satan unto God. It leads us to a complete mortification of our lusts and passions and to a cleanness from all the pollutions of the flesh and spirit. Beware of such zeal, though it call itself a zeal of God, as is not concerned about internal purity, growth in grace, and an obedient walk with God. Let not jangling guides lead you into doubt and confusion.

But one may say, "I have already come to Ije-abarim and find myself in a confusion of ways. I know not which course to take. What shall I do?" The answer of God's Word is that in such a case one is first to stand still and supplicate wisdom from the Holy Spirit, pleading the promise that we "shall be *all* taught of God" (John vi. 45). Secondly, to live in the exercise of true love to all sons of the common Father, and yet not to consort with narrow sects or unchristian parties. Thirdly, to cleave to Christ crucified as the true and only way which leads to life (Luke ix. 23).

Even though the pilgrim know not which way to turn in the confusion of many counsels about minor things, if he hold to this attitude toward Christ he cannot miss salvation. Moreover, in this very process of waiting we grow in grace, and this shall lead us to growth in knowledge and divine illumination. The "pure in heart see God" and at length shall be freed from Ije-abarim.

The state of the pilgrim at this station is variously expressed in Scripture. It is called:

1. *Doubting.*

"Wherefore didst thou doubt?" (Matt. xiv. 31.) The Greek word here contains precisely the idea of Ije-abarim. It is a figurative word, taken from the hesitation and confusion of a person standing at a point where two roads or two fords meet. What a vivid picture of the real essence of doubt! The same word occurs in Matthew xxviii. 17: "But some doubted"—some stood in uncertainty, as does an undecided pilgrim at the cross-roads. There is no need of this. Jesus is our guide as He is our bountiful provider. See His tender appeal in Luke xii. 29: "Neither be ye of doubtful mind" ("Live not in careful suspense," as it is in the marg.). The figure in the Greek word here is of some unstable thing floating in the air; or, as others take it, of a ship tossed about in a storm, now rising and now falling to the tumbling of the waves. Look also at these three texts: Acts x. 20; Romans iv. 20; James i. 6. In these three passages the same Greek word is translated by three different English words: "doubting," "staggering," "wavering."

2. *Double-mindedness.*

"How long halt ye between two opinions [or two *thoughts*]?" (1 Kings xviii. 21.) Dr. Adam Clarke says the idea here is taken from a bird hopping from one twig to another and not knowing on which to settle. Scott regards the figure as taken from the unequal walk of a lame person. In either case it shows vividly the double-mindedness of the Ije-abarim station. "I hate vain thoughts" (Ps. cxix. 113), or, as "vain" is in italics, showing that it is not in the original, we should read, "I hate thoughts." Divided thoughts, distracting thoughts, double thoughts, are an abomination. The one trusting thought of the one law is the only safe guide. "He that is perverse in ways"—in *two* ways—"shall fall at once" (Prov. xxviii. 18). There is no certainty to the man who stands in confusion before the two roads, or tries to walk in both. "No man can serve two masters" (Matt. vi. 24). The apostle desires that the Corinthians "may attend unto the Lord without distraction," without being *drawn in different ways* (1 Cor. vii. 35). This is the literal meaning of the Greek word, as it is of our old English word "distraction." This is exactly the Ije-abarim state of mind, which we are to avoid or escape from in Christ. This is double-mindedness. (See James i. 8, iv. 8).

3. *Double-heartedness.*

This is the real difficulty. "With a double heart do they speak," *an heart and an heart* (Ps. xii. 2). Look at 1 Chronicles xii. 33 and compare the thirty-eighth verse—men of the "double heart" contrasted with those with a "perfect heart," of "one united heart." The right sort is described by the psalmist when he says of the godly man that "his heart is fixed" (Ps. cxii. 7). And David twice says of himself, "My heart is fixed, O God, my heart is fixed" (Ps. lvii. 7). And yet again he says, "My heart is fixed" (Ps. cviii. 1). But of Israel in defection Hosea says, "Their heart is divided" (Hos. x. 2). This is a sad state to be in. It is to be like a cake unturned (Hos. vii. 8), half baked, half dough; it is to be like a "speckled bird," unfit for sacrifice (Jer. xii. 9); it is to be like a city or house or kingdom divided against itself (Matt. xii. 25).

Oh, that we may be the recipients of such blessing

as that described in Ephesians i. 18 (R. V.): "Having the eyes of our *heart* enlightened"! That is the main thing. If we *desire* the light, the light will be given. If we "follow on to know" God and the right ford that leads to God, Ije-abarim will no longer be a place of perplexity to us.

XL.

DIBON-GAD.

It is quite a journey from the last station to this, as will be seen by a reference to the map of the peninsula of Sinai. You will observe that the Israelites are journeying straight northward now along the foot-hills of the mountains of Moab. A charming route it is, full of pleasant pictures to delight the eye—gentle slopes, peaceful valleys, wide pastures, and fertile fields. They pass through several interesting places before reaching Dibon-gad, but for wise reasons these are not mentioned in the thirty-third chapter of Numbers. As has already been indicated, Moses, by special command of God, wrote down the forty-two important stations which contain within themselves a parable of the Christian's journey to the heavenly Canaan. Hence such stopping-places as do not have part in this inspired parable are excluded from this particular enumeration.

This Dibon-gad is a very interesting station on account of its historical associations. In the twenty-first chapter of Numbers we find it mentioned as having been seized upon by the tribe of Gad after the overthrow of the kings, Sihon and Og (Num. xxi. 30). From the circumstance that this town—originally called

Dibon—was captured and rebuilt by the children of Gad, it receives, in the account before us, the compound name of " Dibon-gad." The town stood in the midst of a very rich pastoral country, and very naturally the tribes of Reuben and Gad desired to possess themselves of this region. In the thirty-second chapter of Numbers we have the whole account presented, of how the children of Reuben and the children of Gad came and spoke unto Moses and to Eleazar, the priest, requesting that this fertile pasturage country should be given them for an inheritance. Moses replied that if they would "go up before the people" of the Lord and capture the country, meanwhile defending the Israelites as a vanguard, their request would be granted. Read the whole account in the thirty-second chapter of Numbers, for it is very suggestive of the true spiritual life of conquest. They who take the lead, bear the brunt of battle, and are eager to yield themselves up in true charity and self-sacrifice, receive the inheritance of peace and satisfaction. This is the lesson.

The town of Dibon is mentioned in a number of places in the Scriptures as a "citadel," a "high place of Moab" (Josh. xiii. 9; Isa. xv. 2; Jer. xlviii. 18, 22, 24). There must have been a battle royal when the brave children of Gad advanced against this stronghold of the Moabitish forces. The splendid purpose which was in the hearts of the assailants to prove worthy leaders of the Lord's host was matched by the strong love of country which the people of Moab must have entertained. That the victory was gained by the tribe of Gad shows at once the warlike prowess of these warriors and the divine help freely accorded them.

The meaning of the word "Dibon" is "sufficient knowledge" or "sufficient understanding." This gives to us a very interesting spiritual lesson when taken in contrast with the last station. It will be observed that in the forty-fifth verse of the thirty-third chapter of Numbers the name of the last station is changed, the reading being, "They departed from Iim, and pitched in Dibon-gad." The literal meaning of "Iim" is "doubts," "confusions," or "fluctuations of thought," so that we have here a parable of the journey of the heavenly pilgrim from the place of "doubts" to a position of "sufficient knowledge."

1. Let us inquire first of all *in what this sufficient knowledge consists.* It must impress every pilgrim on the heavenly road that he needs a complete understanding of *self*. This is the first thing we need to know. "The heart is deceitful above all things, and desperately wicked," and out of this heart the self-life grows. Until we have thoroughly studied the heart under the search-light of divine truth, we are constantly under the dominion of doubts and uncertainties; but the Bible wonderfully unfolds self in all its deceptions and dangers, and thus leads us on to our spiritual Dibon. We also need a sufficient knowledge of *sin*, and this the Word of God supplies. We need, in the third place, an understanding of the devices of *Satan*. Here the Word of God is all-important, warning us of our arch-enemy: "Lest Satan should get an advantage of us: for we are not ignorant of his devices" (2 Cor. ii. 11). We may at our spiritual Dibon "put on the whole armor of God" and thus be able to stand against "the wiles [the *subtle methods of deceit*] of the devil." At this

station we find the promise made good to us: "When He, the Spirit of truth, is come, He will guide you into all truth" (John xvi. 13); for "God is faithful, who will not suffer you to be tempted above that ye are able; but will with the temptation also make a way to escape" (1 Cor. x. 13).

2. Notice that this "sufficient knowledge" *comes about through war.* The word "Gad" means "army," "arming," or "military invasion." From this we may learn that the knowledge of self, sin, and Satan which we acquire at our Dibon-gad results from the holy warfare in which we are engaged; from the strife and struggle against defilements of the flesh and spirit, against "principalities, and powers, and the rulers of the darkness of this world, against spiritual wickedness in high places" (Eph. vi. 12). From this warfare results the sufficient knowledge which is such a comfort and source of strength to the warrior.

No one can sincerely take up the weapons against envy, wrath, malice, injustice, and unrighteousness without coming to a larger and deeper appreciation of peace and meekness, faith and love, truth and righteousness.

3. We learn, in the third place, that the *Word of God is the chief weapon in this warfare.* Through the Word we obtain victory and by it are we led to this "sufficient knowledge." The weapons which the Word provides are mighty, through God, to the pulling down of strongholds and to the casting down of evil imaginations, that every high thought may be subject unto the obedience of Christ (2 Cor. x. 4, 5). It is at Dibon-gad that we realize the fulfilment of the blessed promise, "He that hath My commandments, and keepeth them, he it is

that loveth Me: and he that loveth Me shall be loved of My Father, and I will love him, and will manifest Myself to him."

In the midst of the uncertainties of human knowledge and the waverings of human opinions, it is encouraging to look into God's Word and discover *what we know.* Notice the progress in the following passages:

Romans vii. 18: "I know that in me dwelleth no good thing."

1 John iii. 5: "Ye know that He was manifested."

2 Corinthians viii. 9: "Ye know the grace of our Lord Jesus Christ."

1 Peter i. 18, 19: "Ye know that ye were not redeemed with silver and gold, but with blood."

Job xix. 25: "I know that my Redeemer liveth," Job's simple and sufficient creed.

John ix. 25: "One thing I know, that, whereas I was blind, now I see."

1 John iii. 14: "We know that we have passed from death unto life."

2 Timothy i. 12: "I know whom I have believed."

Romans viii. 28: "We know that all things work together for good."

1 John v. 15: "If we know that He hear us, we know that we have."

2 Corinthians v. 1: "We know that we have a building of God, eternal in the heavens."

1 John iii. 2: "We know that we shall be like Him."

This is "sufficient knowledge" indeed! It conducts us straight through the realm of doctrine, straight through the whole of life. It leaves us "like Christ," though it finds us with "no good thing."

XLI

ALMON-DIBLATHAIM

THE last stations of the long journey through the wilderness give to us the very highest experiences of the Christian. We may compare these concluding stopping-places with the last months or years of the aged Christian's life; or they may typify the highest attainments of those who, by entire consecration to the Lord's will and work, are leading absolutely separated lives in His sight. The Epistle to the Ephesians deals throughout with these highest experiences of life and service, and should be studied carefully in this connection.

From the "sufficient knowledge" of self and sin and Satan which we attained at our last station, we go on to a new and even more blessed experience. Almondiblathaim will be seen upon the map straight north from Dibon-gad and just beyond the country of the Amorites. It has been identified in a village still standing just north of the Arnon, and there is every probability that traces of the ancient town will be discovered on further exploration. It is supposed by scholars that the name was given to the place from the circumstance that it was the center of vast rows of fig-trees, whose fruit was very frequently collected and stored there for shipment. "Diblathaim" signifies "cakes" or "lumps of figs," and is used in 1 Samuel xxv. 18. This may be the same town as that mentioned in Jeremiah xlviii. 22, called Beth-diblathaim, which may be rendered "the house of fig-cakes." "Almon," the other word compounded into the name of this station, means "hidden"; so that by building together these various meanings we come to this, that the full name signifies "hidden abundance of figs."

Spiritually we learn from this that God has abundant consolations for those who have made the weary way through the desert and are coming close to Him in full surrender of heart, or in preparation for admittance to heaven. It seems to me that there is a beautiful fitness in the fact that this station follows immediately after Dibon-gad. The "sufficient understanding" which results from spiritual warfare prepares for the great joy and peace in believing, all doubts and fears and confusions having been put away from us. As "the light is sweet, and a pleasant thing it is for the eyes to behold the sun" (Eccles. xi. 7), so is it peculiarly delightful to us when the divine light shines upon our way and our work, the "Sun of righteousness arising upon us with healing in His wings."

There are three main lessons to be learned at this station, as to the consolations which God stands ready to bestow upon all those who come close to Him. They are:

1. *Hidden consolations.*

The refreshments and joys of the kingdom are not known to the world, or to those who give themselves in any large part to the world. "The world seeth Me no more; but ye see Me," said our blessed Lord. Our eyes being fixed upon Him, we find entering quietly into our inmost souls the sweet comforts which His glorified face and risen life bestow. He is the living "Bread which cometh down from heaven" (John vi. 50); He is the true "hidden manna" given to him that is overcoming (Rev. ii. 17). All this we find realized in us when we have come to our spiritual Almon-diblathaim, our "hidden place of figs." We find that our life is "hid with Christ in God" (Col. iii. 3). We are able to say with Him, "We have meat to eat that ye know not of" (John iv. 32). We are nourished by interior subsistence, for our heavenly Guest has come in unto us and has shut to the door, and we are "supping with Him, and He with us" (Rev. iii. 20). (See Ps. xxv. 14; Prov. iii. 32, xiv. 10; Matt. xiii. 11.)

2. *Abundant consolations.*

The cakes or lumps of figs typify the inexhaustible stores of refreshments in God's Word for us. He has provided a feast, and at a feast there is always abundance. The King hath sent forth His servants to cry, "Come, for all things are now ready." "They shall be abundantly satisfied" (Ps. xxxvi. 8); "My servants shall eat, drink, and rejoice" (Isa. lxv. 13). Our blessed Lord Himself stands at the head of the board to say to us, "Eat, O friends; drink, yea, drink abundantly, O beloved" (Song of Sol. v. 1).

3. *Nourishing consolations.*

Figs have ever been noted for the amount of nourishment they contain. Among the promises which God gave to Israel, to animate the people to perseverance and to impel them to hasten on to possess the land, was that they should find it to be the "land of fig-trees" (Deut. viii. 8). Cakes of figs were not only set before guests at their great entertainments (1 Chron. xii. 39, 40), but were employed constantly as daily diet; so that we are taught at this station that God's consolations are designed to nourish and strengthen us. How many feeble hearts have found this to be true!

There is no sweeter thought in all the Scriptures than that of "feeding upon Christ." Notice how it is referred to as the constant and consoling privilege of the Christian. It is set forth in figure by the tree of life (Gen. ii. 9, iii. 22; Rev. xxii. 2; Ezek. xlvii. 12); the paschal lamb (Exod. xii. 8; 1 Cor. v. 7, 8); the manna, that wonderful "spiritual meat" (1 Cor. x. 3), which was truly "angels' food" ("bread of the mighty," Ps. lxxviii. 25, marg., cf. ciii. 20, marg.) and "rained down from heaven" (Exod. xvi. 4); and the showbread, literally "bread of the presence" (Lev. xxiv. 5–9), called the "continual bread" (Num. iv. 7). Oh, the fullness of Christ! Blessed are they that hunger and thirst after Him! They shall feed upon the hidden figs of His grace; they shall be filled with abundant and nourishing consolations. Contrast with this the portion of the carnal and ungodly, who feed on the "wind" (Hos. xii. 1), on "husks" (Luke xv. 16), and on "ashes" (Isa. xliv. 20).

XLII

MOUNTAINS OF ABARIM

WITH deep sighs of relief and with eyes bright with hope, the people now ascend into the mountains of Abarim beyond Heshbon and before Nebo. (See Num. xxxiii. 47.) From these heights they were able to obtain a glimpse of the river Jordan and of the walls of Jericho beyond. They could see something of the Land of Promise itself, stretching away in all its fertile beauty toward the west and north. What thoughts must have thrilled their hearts—thoughts reaching back into the past and on into the future!

The goodness of God in all their way must have impressed them, and the faithfulness of God in fulfilling His promises must have brought glad halleluiahs to their lips.

As will be seen upon the map, the mountains of Abarim are a continuation of the hills of Moab. The highest peak, situated right opposite Jericho, was called Mount Nebo. From the top of this peak Moses was to behold the land of Canaan, and then was to die "at the kiss of Jehovah" (Deut. xxxiv. 5). The word "Abarim" signifies "passages," "passings over," or "passings away." It is supposed by scholars that the name was given from the circumstance that these mountains run down to the fords or passages of Jordan. However that might be, there are certain practical lessons to be drawn from the station which no thoughtful mind can miss. We learn:

1. *The passing away of Moses and the old covenant.*

Up to this time Moses had been the center of God's work with the Israelites in the desert. In his commanding presence he represented the methods of divine Providence through the law and penal ordinances. However, "the law made nothing perfect, but it was the bringing in [or "introduction"] of a better hope" (Heb. vii. 19). It was necessary that the people of Israel come up to the spiritual heights, where they should get a conception of the passing away of the old covenant. How much they grasped of this in the mountains of Abarim we do not know; but certainly God meant to give them a glimpse of this great truth and turn their eyes toward Christ, to whom the law should lead.

2. *The preparation for passing from law to Christ.*

This is one of the lessons which we should learn at our spiritual Abarim: "The law was given by Moses, but grace and truth came by Jesus Christ" (John i. 17). This truth enters more and more into our consciousness as we progress in the separated life. "We are not under the law, but under grace;" we serve not as slaves, but as children; we obey not through force, but through love. The ten commandments remain in binding force upon us, but we keep them through the mighty power of a new motive, that of love to the Father who made the commands and laid them upon us.

3. *The preparation for passing from the observation of the letter to the love of the Spirit—from prophecy to power.*

A great change is to come at the next station: Moses is to pass away; Joshua is to come in as leader and commander. Joshua is the type of Christ, "the power of God," the Lord from heaven, whose cleansing Spirit has been given to us to become *power in us*. All this is prepared for in our spiritual Abarim. Hints of this new covenant we have in many parts of the Old Testament, as, for example, in Jeremiah xxxi. 31. Its full fruition and revelation were reserved for the New Testament. "He hath made the first old. Now that which decayeth and waxeth old is ready to vanish away" (Heb. viii. 13).

These mountains of Abarim may also signify to us those states of exaltation into which God graciously leads the soul as a preparation for death. They were types of the Delectable Mountains from whose summits the pilgrim obtains inspiring glimpses of the New Jerusalem. The sound of the swelling Jordan is in his ears, but he is able to forget the suggestions of terror which it conveys. He must walk down into the valley, but it shall contain only a "shadow of death," not the substance to him. The rod and staff of his divine Joshua shall be his support. The waters shall divide before his feet, and an abundant entrance shall be ministered to him into Immanuel's land.

Altogether our visit to the mountains of Abarim gives to us the thought of *preparation*. This thought is very important. We should prepare for meeting God in the sanctuary, in service, and at the family altar as well as at death and the judgment. The real application of Amos iv. 12, "Prepare to meet thy God," is to the present life, not the future. We are to look ahead and by inward searchings and prayer get ourselves ready for public worship, and especially for the partaking of the elements of the Lord's Supper. It is a solemn thing to "meet with God" under any circumstances. Notice how many times God insists upon the need of preparation before engaging in worship or service (2 Chron. xxxv. 4; 1 Sam. vii. 3; Ezra vii. 10; Job xi. 13; Jer. xlvi. 14; and many other passages). The Jews had a special day of preparation for the partaking of the Passover (Matt. xxvii. 62; John xix. 14). How often God commanded the people to "sanctify themselves" for some special manifestation of power to be displayed upon the morrow! (Exod. xix. 10; Lev. viii. 30; Josh. vii. 13; 2 Chron. xxix. 5; and many other passages.)

See how God has set us an example by preparing duly for all things which He has purposed to bestow in blessing upon His people. It is a mark of the Lord's goodness that He hath prepared the light and the sun (Ps. lxxiv. 16), the gentle showers and the plentiful rain (Ps. lxv. 10, lxviii. 9, 10, cxlvii. 8). He hath also caused the corn to spring up out of the ground prepared for it (Ps. lxv. 9, marg.). In the Book of Jonah we find all things "prepared" for the services they are to render: the fish (i. 17), the gourd (iv. 6), the worm (iv. 7), the vehement east wind (iv. 8), and the wind that caused the tempest (i. 4). So in the work of grace God hath made full preparation. God's "vessels of mercy are afore prepared unto glory" (Rom. ix. 23);

they are "vessels unto honor, prepared unto every good work" (2 Tim. ii. 21); they are "created in Christ Jesus unto good works, which God hath before ordained" (marg., "prepared," Eph. ii. 10); altogether God's people are "a people prepared for the Lord" (Luke i. 17).

In all holy life and service let us remember that "He that hath *wrought* us ["made, fashioned us"] for the selfsame thing is God" (2 Cor. v. 5)—a beautiful text, showing how God hath "prepared," and how we should "prepare," that we may be fully and blessedly co-laborers with God.

XLIII

PLAINS OF MOAB

DOWN from the "delectable mountains" the long procession swept to encamp in the valley. How significant is the forty-eighth verse of the chapter we are studying: "They departed from the mountains of Abarim, and pitched in the plains of Moab by Jordan near Jericho"! Before them were the dangers they had to encounter; behind them were the mountains from whose summits they had obtained wondrous views to inspire them for the contest. What a picture the straggling ranks must have made as, footsore and weary after the forty years' wanderings, they came down to the spacious plains! Their fathers had died in the desert; their flocks and herds had been consumed by the necessities of the weary journeyings. A new generation of people faced Jordan, and new flocks and herds had sprung up around them. How eager the people must have been to pass over into Palestine and enjoy the promised rest! Before this could be, however, there was much training of heart and conscience to be undergone. The descent to the plains of Moab is an indication of the deep humiliation into which God saw it necessary for them to enter. This is numerically the forty-second journey, and, as has already been indicated, the number forty-two typifies in Scripture the whole period of spiritual training and trial through which God causes a nation or a church, or the church or an individual, to pass. In the thirteenth chapter of Revelation, at the fifth verse, we read that to the wild beast " coming up out of the sea " there was given power to afflict the church forty and two months. This agrees with the " time, and times, and half a time," i.e., the three years and a half, during which the church, on two wings of a great eagle, escaped to the wilderness to be tempted of Satan and nourished by God (Rev. xii. 14). In other parts of the Scriptures one thousand two hundred and sixty days are mentioned as the period of training (Rev. xii. 6), and it will be noticed that this agrees with the number of days in the forty-two months. Consequently in the station before us, being the forty-second of the journeying, we are shown the completion of the wanderings and discipline under which Israel was prepared for Canaan. We have seen the people passing through every conceivable experience. They need now to pause for a time in the valley of humiliation before crossing over into the land flowing with milk and honey; they need space for quiet thought and faithful self-examination. Three dispensations preliminary to perfect fitness for Canaan are clearly brought before us in this station:

1. *The drawing dispensation.*

They were still under the leadership of Moses, whose name signifies " drawing " or " a drawer." The child had been drawn out of the river Nile, to be adopted by the daughter of Pharaoh; as a man he had become a " drawer " to take the people out of Egypt. Having drawn them forth from the entanglements of Goshen and from the dangers and perplexities of the desert, he was now preparing to turn them over into the hands of Joshua as their chief leader. Hence up to this time we may see in type the dispensation of drawing wherein the Father wooes us away from the world and its entanglements, in order that we may submit ourselves unto Jesus, our divine Joshua. "No man can come to Me, except the Father which hath sent Me draw him" (John vi. 44). It is thought by some that the Saviour had in mind the desert dispensation when uttering these words, and that His saying which immediately follows, "I will raise him up at the last day," is a reference to the passage of Jordan, by which Israel escaped from the wilderness and came into the resurrection life of Canaan. However this may be, we are authorized to learn here the lesson that God sweetly draws the soul unto its strong Joshua, to submit to Him in all things, and receive His indwelling and governing Spirit.

It will be seen that this implies something of a change in the interpretation to be put upon this last station of the desert wanderings. The plains of Moab may properly stand for those experiences which lead the soul to perfect surrender to Christ, death to the world and to sin, and a new life in the Spirit comparable to the pleasures and possessions of Canaan. Taken as a whole, the desert wandering typifies, as we have seen, the entire earthly life of the believer. It shows us the Christian's pilgrimage through the world, until, sanctified and made fit, he is at death received into the promised habitations. But the experiences of Israel in this last station, the plains of Moab, typify the struggles, temptations, hopes, fears, and final surrender of the half-hearted Christian by which he enters upon the fully consecrated resurrection life.

What Paul describes in the seventh chapter of Romans may be regarded as the fluctuating state of the soul in the spiritual plains of Moab. What he so gloriously portrays in the eighth chapter is the full consecration of the Canaan life. Death in Jordan and resurrection upon the other bank are means thereto. If we bear this in mind we will see an instructive type of that drawing work which God the Father does in wooing us out of our doubts and dangers into the fullness of trust and the peace of the blessed life.

For all of this we are prepared in Abarim, and into it we more fully come in the station we are now studying. The order of the soul's progress is very well expressed by the Saviour in Matthew xxviii. 19, where He says, "Go ye therefore, and teach all nations, baptizing them in [or rather "into"] the name of the Father, and of the Son, and of the Holy Ghost." This baptizing into the name of the Father corresponds with that preliminary dispensation which is typified in the whole period when Moses, the "drawer," was leading the Israelites to perfect surrender to Joshua. It began when they followed Moses through the Red Sea. "They were all baptized unto [or "into"] Moses in the cloud and in the sea" (1 Cor. x. 2). It is completed, as we shall see, in the hardships and soul struggles in the valleys over which Nebo towered then, and towers still, so gloriously.

2. *The submissive dispensation.*

Of this we obtain a glimpse as we pause here for the present in the plains of Moab. Israel was to come into perfect submission to Joshua. The lot that had befallen them in the weary journey was preparatory thereto; particularly were they to experience the humiliations of the plains of Moab, in order that they might yield themselves body and soul unto their new leader. In like manner are we led into submission to the Son of God.

Thus are we baptized "into the name of the Son," which typifies that we are willing to follow His leading through life and through death in total submission. Thus are we baptized into the likeness of His death and resurrection, passing with Him through Jordan, and marching with Him into the resurrection life of Canaan. Oh, sweet and encouraging submission to our loving Saviour! "Take My yoke upon you, and learn of Me." Who would not joyously obey such a command?

3. *The dispensation of love.*

We may pause a moment longer to notice that we are also to be baptized through Jordan "into the name of the Holy Ghost." "The end of the commandment is love out of a pure heart, and of a good conscience, and of faith unfeigned" (1 Tim. i. 5).

This is the dispensation of the Holy Spirit, who is a Spirit of love, and when we submit ourselves wholly unto Him we have received that enduement of power for service which every Christian so greatly needs.

Sufficient weight is not given to the fact that God's Holy Spirit is a Spirit of love. We believe that God the Father *is* love, and that He "so loved the world that He gave His only begotten Son." We believe our Saviour's words when He says, "My Father will love him, and I will love him." But we forget how many times the love of the Holy Ghost is referred to in Scripture. Paul writes to the Romans, "Now I beseech you, brethren, by our Lord Jesus Christ, and by the love of the Spirit, that ye strive together with me in your prayers" (Rom. xv. 30, R. V.). The thought of love is connected with the Holy Spirit in the following passages: 2 Corinthians vi. 6; Galatians v. 22; Philippians ii. 1; Colossians i. 8; and many others. The completeness of the Christian life and consecration will be brought about only when the heart has been truly baptized into the Father, the Son, and the Holy Ghost. All fear is then cast out by love, and the whole renewed creature is subdued unto Him, that the triune God may be all in all (1 John iv. 18; 1 Cor. xv. 28).

XLIV

PLAINS OF MOAB—PITCHING BEFORE JORDAN

We read that the Israelites pitched by Jordan near Jericho, or, as it is in the Hebrew, "by Jordan of Jericho." They are now facing the historic river which meant so much to them and will ever mean so much to the Christian. They stood fronting the plunge into perfect trust, and they shivered and shrank, as almost every child of God does under like circumstances. The Bible is full of references to the Jordan. Lot chose the plain of Jordan for his residence (Gen. xiii. 11). From his day onward the river is associated with the lives of kings and princes, herdsmen and tillers of the soil. In our hymnology the Jordan usually means death, and it may be thus used quite properly. Let us grasp the greater lesson along with the lesser,—the lesson already hinted at,—that the passing through the Jordan may mean to us a baptism into the larger and higher life. Pitching beside the river to-day, we may learn seven lessons:

1. *The meaning of Jordan.*

The word literally signifies "the sending forth of judgment." This is the interpretation put upon it by Bromley and others. Certain scholars, however, derive it from a word which signifies "descending," "humiliation," "being humble." You will observe in the concordance that Cruden gives both of these interpretations. The spiritual lessons which we may rightly draw would be about the same in either case. He who steps into the river of judgment will inevitably feel the effects of such an experience in true humility of heart. Judgment of self and sin under the search-light of the Word is included in the utter yielding to the Spirit. True repentance is one condition leading to the reception of the Holy Ghost.

2. *The swelling of Jordan.*

Jeremiah asks, "How wilt thou do in the swelling of Jordan?" (Jer. xii. 5.) This is a manifest allusion to the mighty floods which sometimes swept through this river's course, making great noise and roaring. These floods are used as emblems of special judgments coming upon sin in us at different times during our lives. To lead us to self-surrender God will deal sharply with the evil that lurks in us. "The Spirit lusts against the flesh." We should stand aside and let the fires of God burn; let the floods of Jordan sweep through our hearts to cleanse them! This is one lesson. We must not forget that the swelling of Jordan also typifies the overflowing of judgment upon the ungodly at death. Isaiah makes reference to this when he quotes God as saying, "When thou passest through the waters, I will be with thee; and through the rivers, they shall not overflow thee" (Isa. xliii. 2). The wicked shall be overthrown, but the righteous shall pass safely through the dark waters. As Israel pitched beside the Jordan their minds must have been vividly impressed by the thought of those special judgments as shown in the afflictions and difficulties through which they had already passed. Strange that they did not learn to avoid those sins which were yet to bring bitter results upon them!

3. *The baptism of Jordan.*

The waters were parted, and yet as the people marched through there was typified a baptism of suffering which is frequently referred to in Scripture. "As many of us as were baptized into Christ were baptized into His death." As Jordan implies judgment and humiliation, so we through our difficulties should learn to humble ourselves as under the rod of the righteous judgment of God, to submit our wills unto Him, to cultivate true poverty of spirit, and so to improve all chastisements of His rod that we may come at length into the land of peace. "Are ye able to be baptized with the baptism wherewith I am baptized?" Let us cultivate a spirit that will enable us to say more truly than John and James could at first say, "We are able."

4. *The overflowing of Jordan.*

It is further said that the Israelites encamped by Jordan of Jericho. This latter was a city of the Canaanites, on the border of whose land the river flowed. Jericho was a wicked city, hence devoted to destruction. Jericho had apparently appropriated the Jordan in a special sense as its own. "The Jordan of Jericho" was doubtless an expression much used at the time. This may teach us how cities and individuals unconsciously appropriate judgment to themselves; it may show the nearness and readiness of God's power to punish sin. Annually the Jordan overflowed at the time of harvest (Josh. iii. 15). Signally and suddenly God's judgment, as a mighty flood, has often overwhelmed the nations. "When they shall say, Peace and safety; then sudden destruction cometh upon them" (1 Thess. v. 3). Moreover, the time of harvest represents the end of the world, as our Lord Himself teaches us (Matt. xiii. 39). Therefore, camping by the river to-day, we should not fail to learn the lesson of divine judgment, whether it come to us soon after our sin or tarry till the last day.

5. *The partings at Jordan.*

Partings beside the river, oh, how many there have occurred! Husband from wife, wife from husband, parents from children. The brink of Jordan is the saddest spot in all the earthly pilgrimage; sadder than the place where the two ways met and Orpah turned back to her people.

And there is something sadder for us to think of here than the partings caused by death: the partings resulting from apostasy. In the forty-ninth verse of the chapter we are studying, the thirty-third of Numbers, Moses gives a more particular description of this last station by describing the limits of the camp: "They pitched by Jordan, from Beth-jesimoth even unto Abel-shittim in the plains of Moab." These details are extremely significant. It is interesting to observe that this place or city called Beth-jesimoth was situated in the most fertile part of the plains of Moab, and was allotted to the Reubenites by Moses (Josh. xiii. 15-20).

Yet the name "Beth-jesimoth" signifies "the house of desolation." This is singular when the fertility of that portion of the plain is taken into account, but the meaning is that, though the plain was fertile, a residence upon it produced spiritual desolation. This was because of its nearness to the Moabites, who were an idolatrous nation and brought desolation upon Israel in this station by seducing them to their iniquities. This is fully described in the Book of Numbers from the twenty-second to the twenty-fifth chapters. We shall have occasion to study these lessons later.

6. *The meetings at Jordan.*

If there be sad partings through apostasy or through death beside the river, there are also glorious meetings upon the other bank. "The king returned, and came to Jordan" (2 Sam. xix. 15). Our King has promised to return and meet us at Jordan (John xiv. 3). "They two stood by Jordan" (2 Kings ii. 7). How sweetly will we be able to say the same when Christ or our loved ones meet us beside the river! What language can describe the meetings of faithful hearts, after earth's siftings and separations, when severed friendships shall be reknit, and loves that seem so rudely broken shall be reëstablished for eternity!

7. *The victory over Jordan.*

Zechariah exclaims joyfully, "The pride of Jordan is spoiled" (Zech. xi. 3). The psalmist cried, "The sea fled: Jordan was driven back" (Ps. cxiv. 3). These expressions of triumph are only feebly typical of the glorious victories which Christ has given over death and the grave. "O death, where is thy sting? O grave, where is thy victory? Thanks be to God, which giveth us the victory through our Lord Jesus Christ" (1 Cor. xv. 55, 57). How often the expression is used in the Bible, "They passed clean through [or "over"]

Jordan"! This describes exactly the glorious triumph which the true Christian experiences in the moment of death. It also hints at the peace of those who resolutely pass clean through the baptism of self-surrender and stand with Christ upon the banks of the Canaan life. Let us not stop with anything less than this.

XLV

PLAINS OF MOAB—IN CONTACT WITH THE MOABITES

WE must give particular attention to the temptations which a residence near the Moabites caused the people of Israel. A full account of their contact with this idolatrous nation is given us in the twenty-fifth chapter of Numbers. Indeed, we must go back to the twenty-second chapter of Numbers, and consider the whole story of Balak's conspiracy and Balaam's prophecy, if we are to have the complete picture. It was while the people were encamped beside Jordan, with Beth-jesimoth at one limit of their tents and Abel-shittim at the other, that these significant transactions took place. Very sore trials and many alluring temptations come to those who are meditating the plunge into the Jordan of self-surrender.

We have already seen that "Beth-jesimoth" signifies "the house of desolation," and it is necessary for us to observe that "Abel-shittim" means "the sorrow of scourges." This latter place seems to have been so named because of the sin of Israel and the consequent sorrow which fell upon the people in that place. The wrath of God was awakened against them, and twenty-four thousand of their number were cut off (Num. xxv. 9). How significant, therefore, was the position of the

Israelites at this point of their progress! On one extreme "the house of desolation," and on the other "the sorrow of scourges"! Mournfully the saying of James comes to us, "When lust hath conceived, it bringeth forth sin; and sin, when it is finished, bringeth forth death" (James i. 15).

Studying carefully the twenty-fifth chapter of Numbers, we learn at least seven important lessons:

1. *Spiritual unfaithfulness.*

The sin of the men of Israel with the daughters of Moab typifies that unfaithfulness which the Word of God frequently charges against those who depart in their love and truth from the service of the Master. James exclaims, "Whosoever would be a friend of the world maketh himself an enemy of God" (James iv. 4, R. V.). And to this friendliness with the world he attaches the dreadful thought of spiritual unfaithfulness under the figure of adultery: "Ye adulteresses, know ye not," etc. Study the fearful indictment of Israel God makes, through Hosea, under the parable of an adulterous wife (Hos. i.–iv.). The whole teaching here is of spiritual unfaithfulness.

2. *Idolatry.*

The people of Israel "joined themselves" to Baalpeor (Num. xxv. 3). They actually attached themselves in spirit and sympathy to the filthy idol, a full account of whose iniquities we have preserved in both sacred and secular history. Self-love and pride were at the bottom of it, as usual; the egotistic "I" is ever the first letter in idolatry. "Ephraim is joined to idols: let him alone," saith the Lord. The wandering prodigal "joined himself to a citizen" of the far country; he "pinned himself" to the skirts of the alien. This was a large part of his helplessness and misery. In our idolatry of the world, of the almighty dollar, or of the fashions of the time, we are literally joining ourselves unto the enemies of God. This is the root idea of all idolatry. What folly for the child of God to link himself with a tinsel-trapped image that hath no power to hear prayer or to save, nay, that by the very sordidness of the association can only lead astray!

3. *The temptations of Satan.*

Balaam appearing here to tempt Israel unto sin is a very vivid type of Satan, who comes to us in friendly guise, but with malice in his heart. The name "Balaam" literally means "a devourer" or "destroyer of the people," and in that, as in all that he attempts to do, he is a type of the great deceiver who is allowed strange privileges as the prince of this world. Notice that Satan is represented as a "devourer" in Revelation xii. 4. How eager is Satan to impede the steps of the soul on its way to the baptism of self-surrender!

4. *Temptations to worldliness.*

In the leading away of Israel by the fascinations of the surrounding life, how fully do we behold images of the gradual drifting into worldliness of which so many Christians are guilty! At first they could see no harm, doubtless, in associating with the Moabites; those who warned them of their danger were set down as extremists and old fogies. At first the conversations were entirely innocent, and such amusements as were offered seemed quite inoffensive. What harm could there be? Gradually their minds were blinded until they could not see at all. Then headlong they plunged into "the sorrows of the scourges," typified in Abel-shittim. Alas, how frequently has it been the same since their day! There is all too much *drifting* in this generation. "Therefore we ought to give the more earnest heed to the things that were heard, lest haply we *drift away* from them" (Heb. ii. 1, R. V.).

5. *Temptations to the self-life.*

These also are outlined to us in the sad events and scenes enacted before us. The apostle prophesies that in the last days men shall be "lovers of their own selves" (2 Tim. iii. 2), or "lovers of self," as it is in the Revised Version. With what sad literalness has this prophecy been fulfilled! How carefully should we note any tendency to repose too much confidence in ourselves, or in any person or thing, save God, our Saviour! "Having no confidence in the flesh" is put down by St. Paul as one of the three marks by which the members of the true circumcision may be infallibly known (Phil. iii. 3).

6. *Scourges follow yieldings.*

Inevitably must the feet of those who stray from God come at length within the portals of Abel-shittim. "The wages of sin is death" (Rom. vi. 23). The experiences of every leader must have intensified this impression upon mind and heart. Let us be careful that we take lesson from past punishments to avoid future sinning. God will not give us over to our own devices without a struggle. In infinite mercy He "scourgeth every son whom He receiveth," in order that that son may come into the blessed life of peace.

7. *True repentance means turning from sin.*

It is not enough to weep and lament over our transgressions. The Israelites did this, yet the wrath of God was not stayed (Num. xxv. 6). They were required to turn absolutely from their sins, and in addition to this, Phinehas in true zeal was required to put Zimri and Cozbi to death (Num. xxv. 7, 8). The principal offenders needed to be executed before the plague would cease. It is worthy of note that the name "Cozbi" signifies "deceit." Thus it is by deceit and subtlety that the Midianitish woman has always ensnared the foolish heart. The central thought of repentance all through the Scripture is a "turning from," or "forsaking," sin. True repentance is not feeling sorry, but *acting* sorry. Study the whole of the twenty-fifth chapter of Numbers to learn this great lesson. The body of sin must be destroyed, that henceforth we shall not serve sin.

XLVI

PLAINS OF MOAB—IN CONFLICT WITH THE MIDIANITES

WHILE encamped in the plains of Moab God gave the command to Moses which we have in the thirty-first chapter of Numbers, at the second verse: "Avenge the children of Israel of the Midianites." This seems singular, and yet we must remember that God has a right to avenge Himself and to see that His people are avenged: "Vengeance is Mine; I will repay, saith the Lord." Such is the claim which God makes for Himself, and thus at once is His right to vengeance established.

This war against the Midianites was to be one of the last services which Moses might render to the people. God says to him, "Afterward shalt thou be gathered unto thy people" (Num. xxxi. 2). It was among the most distinguished of the services which Moses rendered, and we should study carefully the whole of the thirty-first chapter of Numbers to learn its importance and to derive from it spiritual lessons. Surely when we are encamped in our spiritual plains of Moab we will be subjected to such warfare as is here pictured. May we secure similar commanding victories! We learn much of value both as to our internal and our external conflicts.

1. *The internal conflict.*

Here we may learn many important particulars of the needed battle against the spirit of strife and contention in our own hearts. Notice:

(*a*) The meaning of the word. The word "Midianite" signifies "strife" or "contention." The root from which the word comes is employed in Proverbs xviii. 18: "The lot causeth *contentions* to cease." Consequently we may see in the war against the Midianites the whole struggle against the contentious spirit typified. Pride rises in our hearts, criticisms follow, strifes ensue, and very soon we find ourselves involved in turmoils and inward contentions.

(*b*) The universality of the work. By studying carefully the thirty-first chapter of Numbers we learn how universal the battle against inward strife is. The fourth verse says, "Of every tribe a thousand, throughout all the tribes of Israel, shall ye send to the war." There was no discharge in that war. Not one tribe could plead exemption. Every tribe must be represented by its thousand. So it is with us. We must all plead guilty to the possession within us of the works of the flesh, among which Paul enumerates "strife and seditions" (Gal. v. 20). These must be resisted, mortified, and cut off.

(*c*) The necessities of the war. Moses commanded, "Arm yourselves" (verse 3); "Go" (verse 3); "Sanctify yourselves" (verse 6). The same commands are given to us in all spiritual battles. We are to take unto ourselves "the whole armor of God" (Eph. vi. 13). We are to advance against the enemy with resoluteness and faith. In order to do this, we may pray that we be "sanctified" by the Spirit of the God of battle.

(*d*) The completeness of the work. They slew the kings of Midian as well as the people of Midian, and they cut off Balaam, the son of Beor (Num. xxxi. 8). They left not a single male member of the tribe alive. From this we learn what God requires of us when we undertake to war against evil principles within us. God will have us cut off all the enemy, root and branch. He has Himself pronounced judgment against the spirits of strife and contention in the Christian's heart: "Unto them that are contentious, and do not obey the truth, but obey unrighteousness, indignation and wrath, tribulation and anguish, shall fall upon every soul of man that doeth evil" (Rom. ii. 8, 9). The spirit of strife in the heart is opposite to, and most destructive of, the gospel peace with its meek and quiet fruits. For "the wisdom that is from above is first pure, then peaceable" (James iii. 17). "If any nourish bitter envying [or "bitter zeal"] and strife in their hearts, this wisdom descendeth not from above, but is earthly, sensual, devilish."

(*e*) The results of the work. From the spoiling of the Midianites the people returned with captives and prey and much treasure (Num. xxxi. 12). The spoils typify the glorious results which come to the heart through victory over self. What treasures of peace, of joy in the Holy Ghost, of power with God and with men, are taken by us when we faithfully arm ourselves to battle against inward strifes and contentions!

2. *The external conflict.*

Not only do we need to war against inward adversaries, but we are required to fight against the principalities and powers in the world around us and on the spiritual heights above us.

(*a*) These adversaries are numerous. In the plains of Moab the people of Israel found many enemies. First of all there were the remaining heathen nations, who allured them into unfaithfulness and sin. Then there were subtler foes within their own ranks and in the circle of their acquaintance. Doubtless friendship was used then as now to lead the hearts of the more timid astray. The beauty of woman's smile and the magnetism of the strong man's person were employed to work mischief. And then there was the great enemy, Balaam, who was constantly about looking for opportunities of evil and plotting trouble.

These many enemies, some of them being within the household and apparently within the very church of Israel, reveal to us how numerous our adversaries are in the wide domain of the world.

(*b*) These adversaries are subtle. Moses was wroth against the captains of the host because they had not slain the deceitful women who had led Israel astray. "These caused the children of Israel to commit trespass against the Lord" (Num. xxxi. 16). They should therefore have been destroyed, even as the sinful Cozbi, the daughter of Zur, had been destroyed. But by their very subtlety and witchery of manner, and doubtless by their beauty of face, they had appealed even to the captains, and hence wrongfully they had been preserved alive. Balaam also was very subtle, for we read that these women acted "through the counsel of Balaam" (verse 16). Here we have a hint of the subtleties of our adversaries. Satan is the serpent, and is able to impart much of his serpentine wisdom and slyness to his followers. How much do we need to avail ourselves of the wisdom of God in the battle against our soul enemies!

(*c*) These adversaries shall be overcome. All through the Bible there are promises of victory. As, at the command of Moses, all who had caused Israel to sin were slain with the sword (Num. xxxi. 17, 18), so shall those who oppose themselves to the brethren of Christ be overthrown. Even Balaam, the "devourer," shall die. "The God of peace shall bruise Satan under your feet shortly [or "swiftly"]" (Rom. xvi. 20). The main part of the Book of Revelation, after its real action begins in the sixth chapter, is concerned with the judgments of the seven seals, the seven trumpets, and the seven vials. All of these simply typify righteous judgments upon all the adversaries of the church. In the mysterious chapters of the Book of Revelation, therefore, as everywhere else in God's Word, the Christian finds sweet encouragement of victory.

(*d*) The results of these external conflicts. Most significant are the lessons which we learn from the concluding verses of the thirty-first chapter of Numbers. 1. There are lessons along the line of purification (verses 19–21). When we conquer in any battle of outward sin, one inevitable result is that, through God's grace and Spirit, we become more pure within. 2. There are lessons along the line of preparation (verses 23, 24). The day of fire is coming; let us so build that our works shall "abide the fire." 3. There are lessons along the line of partition (verse 27). "As his part is that goeth down to the battle, so shall his part be that tarrieth by the stuff."

" They also serve who only stand and wait."

When we overcome Satan for ourselves we to that extent help the next man in his conflict with him. Not only do we help him by our example, but we have so far forth weakened the power of the adversary.

XLVII

PLAINS OF MOAB—THE REPETITION OF THE LAW

WHILE encamped in the plains Moses repeated the law, with some additions and with most loving application to the details of the life that Israel might expect in Canaan. This repetition of the law is contained in the Book of Deuteronomy, one of the most thrilling, as it is one of the most touching, books of the Bible. The Hebrews called it "the repetition of the law" and "the book of reprehensions." This indicates their view of it. The object of this restatement of the law was to produce obedience on the part of the people. The key-thought of the whole book we have in the solemn appeal which Moses made: "I call heaven and earth to record this day against you, that I have set before you life and death, blessing and cursing: therefore choose life, that both thou and thy seed may live" (Deut. xxx. 19). Two important lessons are brought before us by this action of Moses in rehearsing the law:

1. *Obedience in general.*

Notice that obedience is exactly the same in all dispensations. Faith has changed somewhat since the time of the patriarchs. They looked forward to a

Christ to come; we look back to one who has already lived and died. Faith with them was expectancy, with us it is the certainty of trust. Hope also has changed from mere anticipation to glorious assurance. So of many other things. We may even say that love has changed somewhat—at least in the matter of becoming purer and deeper—in these latter times. But obedience is exactly the same thing as when the race began. Upon our first parents it was imposed in as complete and binding form as it is required of us. It has suffered no development as the ages have passed. Moses states its terms in his day in the words, "That we love the Lord our God, obey His voice, and cleave unto Him" (Deut. xxx. 20).

This is precisely the same thing that Christ afterward demanded. "Not every one that saith unto Me, Lord, Lord, shall enter into the kingdom of heaven; but he that doeth the will of My Father which is in heaven" (Matt. vii. 21). We find Joshua, the great type of Christ, giving a solemn charge of obedience to Israel before his death, and thus renewing the covenant between God and them, which he summarized in his own practice and expressed in his heroic words, "As for me and my house, we will serve the Lord" (Josh. xxiv. 15). Of Abraham God said, "I know him, that he will command his children and his household after him, and they shall keep the way of the Lord, to do justice and judgment" (Gen. xviii. 19). This shows that obedience with Abraham, as with Noah and Joshua, was the same in character and extent as that which is required of us to-day. It is the binding principle of the faithful heart to God in all ages. The psalmist expresses it thus: "The secret of the Lord is with them that fear Him; and His covenant to make them know it" (Ps. xxv. 14, marg.). Solomon says, "His secret is with the righteous" (Prov. iii. 32).

This is but another way of saying that God speaks, or has discourse, with the renewed, simple, and upright heart. " He made known His *ways* unto Moses;" that is, He explained His plans and unfolded His purposes to the holy and obedient man so dear to Him. But He made known only "His *acts*," His mere outward workings, unto the children of Israel in general. "The Lord spake unto Moses face to face, as a man speaketh unto his friend" (Exod. xxxiii. 11). The reason for this is given in that honorable testimony which Moses received, that he was faithful in all God's house (Num. xii. 7). This confiding discourse into our secret hearts is the reward of obedience. The Lord whispered into Samuel's ear what He had determined to do concerning Saul (1 Sam. ix. 15, marg.). To those who do His will Jesus said, "Henceforth I call you not servants; for the servant knoweth not what his lord doeth: but I have called you friends [or "confidants"]; for all things that I have heard of My Father I have made known unto you" (John xv. 15).

2. *Obedience in particular.*

There are several forms of obedience.

(*a*) Unthinking obedience. There are some who obey God in a mere haphazard sort of way. Jesus asks them if they are able to drink of His cup and be baptized with His baptism, and they, with John and James, cry mechanically, "We are able!" They make great professions when entering upon the Christian life.

They say, as Israel did before the burning mountain, "All that the Lord hath commanded us we will do." We find that, like the Israelites, these over-confident young Christians fall soon into error, disobedience, and despair. In this connection, how touching is the cry of God, "Oh that there were such a heart in them, that they would fear Me, and keep all My commandments always!" (Deut. v. 29.) Obedience is better than sacrifice. (See 1 Sam. xv. 22; Jer. vii. 22, 23; Hos. vi. 6; Micah vi. 6–8.)

(*b*) Coerced obedience. There are some who will not obey God until they are forced by dire afflictions or grievous losses so to do. They are like David at one period of his life, who in times of prosperity followed his own devices and rebelled against God; but when his child was taken from him, when his truly beloved son rose in opposition against him, then David was forced into penitence, driven to obedience. There are many Christians like him. As St. Francis caused the refractory monk to be buried alive to the loins, to the breast, to the very lips, before he would submit, so is it necessary for God to overwhelm some of His children with afflictions and trials before they will yield to the divine will. How much better for us to surrender spontaneously, lovingly, and at once to the will of Him who doeth all things well! The obedience of *children* is the right sort (1 Pet. i. 14), given out of love, and not because the lash of the slave-master has descended upon us. Note that the same Hebrew word is used for "to hear" and "to obey." In Greek the same word is used for unbelief and disobedience. (See John iii. 36; Acts xiv. 2; cf. Rom. ii. 8; 1 Pet. ii. 7, 8.)

(c) Intelligent obedience. This is a higher kind. It counts the cost, and yet is willing to enter upon the building of the tower. It rightly estimates the army of the enemy, and yet is willing to advance to the battle. I suspect that Peter came to the point of intelligent obedience when Jesus said to him, after the resurrection: "If I will that he tarry till I come, what is that to thee? follow thou Me." This meant trial and persecution and death to the apostle, yet he determined to obey. This was the kind of obedience that Paul always manifested after that first supreme cry of his converted heart: "Lord, what wilt Thou have me to do?" Intelligent obedience, Paul-like and Christ-like, is plainly demanded of Christians to-day. Note the remarkable expression: "The obedience of faith" (Rom. xvi. 26). In the chapters between John xiii. and John xvii., obedience is made *seven times* the test of intelligent fellowship with Christ.

(d) Uncommanded obedience. This is the highest attainable kind. It means that we are to be so in love with God, so in sympathy with Him, that even though uncommanded we will obey. As a loving child anticipates the desires of the parent, so will we be eager to do whatsoever shall please our God. A beautiful type of this we find in the example of David's three mighty men of valor. When confined within the stronghold, David breathed a sigh for a cup of water from the well at the gateway of Bethlehem. He did not command the three mighty men to procure it for him, but uncommanded they obeyed. They burst their way through the enemy's ranks, and in much danger to themselves brought to the king the coveted drink.

Oh, that we might be in such close touch and such loving sympathy with Jesus, our King, that we shall know and do His will in all the details of our lives, although that will is not distinctly expressed! It is a grievous sign of lack of sympathy to find Christians constantly perplexed as to what to do and what not to do, what to give up and what to take up. If the life that we now live were wholly the life of Christ, our joy of service would show unerringly where the path of duty lies. Notice, in Psalm ciii. 20, how the highest and noblest obedience comes about when dignity and power are associated with meekness and submission. And see the progress between "doing His commandments," "hearkening unto the voice of His word," and —highest step of all—" doing His pleasure" even without a command (Ps. ciii. 20, 21). With such a temper of mind even "a bird's nest in the way" has sacredness (Deut. xxii. 6, 7).

XLVIII

PLAINS OF MOAB—THE INVESTITURE OF JOSHUA

ANOTHER very important event took place while the people were encamped beside the Jordan and before Beth-peor. This was the final setting apart of Joshua to lead in the people to the Promised Land. A full account of this important ceremony we have in Numbers, the twenty-seventh chapter, from the fifteenth verse to the end. Joshua was to be the successor of Moses, and thus we learn that the law was the schoolmaster to lead to Christ. Joshua had been the minister of Moses, thus being in subordination to him and trained by him (Exod. xvii. 9, xxiv. 13). The whole period of this preliminary training of Joshua shows the humiliation of Christ before His entering upon His divine mission as the Saviour; typifies the training of the church in the Old Testament dispensation, and also shows the state of the soul before it is fully surrendered to Christ, that He may be formed within, the hope of glory.

Certain lessons may be learned from this investiture as to our leader Jesus, and our duty of absolute obedience to Him.

1. *Moses prays for a man* (Num. xxvii. 16): "Let the Lord, the God of the spirits of all flesh, set a man over the congregation."

How vividly this reminds us of the promise of Isaiah: "A man shall be as a hiding-place from the wind, and a covert from the tempest; as rivers of water in a dry place, as the shadow of a great rock in a weary land"! (Isa. xxxii. 2.) That *God* might be all this to the people was no new thought; but that a *man* should be this was a startling prophecy. It was fulfilled in the man Christ Jesus, whom Joshua, the man prayed for by Moses, typified. The humanity of our blessed Lord, thus brought before us, is a precious and encouraging thought. We cannot dwell too much upon His manliness, tenderness, sympathy, oneness with us at "all points." (Note carefully Heb. ii. 14, 16, 17.)

2. *Moses prays for a leader* (verse 17): "May lead them out, that the congregation of the Lord be not as sheep which have no shepherd."

As Joshua was indeed the leader of the people, he forms in that a fitting type of Jesus, the Shepherd of the sheep. Notice that Jesus is called the good Shepherd (John x. 11-18), the great Shepherd (Heb. xiii. 20), and the chief Shepherd (1 Pet. v. 4). These three expressions are extremely significant when we notice that the first is applied to the Shepherd who *dies*, the second to the Shepherd who *rises again* from the dead, and the third to the Shepherd who is to *come again* in glorious majesty.

3. *God's response in the individual* (verse 18): "Take thee Joshua the son of Nun, a man in whom is the spirit, and lay thine hand upon him."

Freely God indicated the one to be chosen, and freely did God devote His own Son to fulfil the type, to become the leader and commander of His people.

4. *God's response made clear in the sight of the congregation* (verse 19): "Set him before Eleazar the priest, and before all the congregation; and give him a charge in their sight."

Thus was Joshua to be set apart, and thus in the fullness of time was Jesus made, in the sight of the high priest and all the people, the propitiation of our sins, and the leader of the church into glory.

5. *God's direction as to a division of honor* (verse 20): "Thou shalt put some of thine honor upon him, that all the congregation of the children of Israel may be obedient."

Thus God shares His honor with the Son: "I receive not honor from men" (John v. 41); "That all men should honor the Son, even as they honor the Father" (John v. 23).

6. *God's direction as to the judgment of Urim* (verse 21): "He shall stand before Eleazar the priest, who shall ask counsel for him after the judgment of Urim before the Lord."

The added honor is given to Jesus in the fact that no Eleazar needs to stand between Him and the wisdom of God. The Father "hath committed all judgment unto the Son" (John v. 22). In this Jesus transcends the type, and becomes to us and to all men the Joshua to lead us, and also the Eleazar, or High Priest, to intercede for us.

7. *The results of the investiture* (verses 22, 23): "Moses did as the Lord commanded him: . . . and he laid his hands upon him, and gave him a charge."

Thus the actual transaction was completed, but of the results we read in Joshua xxi. 44: "There stood not a man of all their enemies before them; the Lord delivered all their enemies into their hand." Victory over sin is the proof that we are in Christ, and that Christ, our Joshua, is in us.

We should make a careful study of Leviticus xvi. and Hebrews ix. in order to see how fully Christ has become our victorious High Priest. The holy of holies was the type of heaven, for therein rested the symbol of the divine glory. Into this the high priest entered once a year. He was clad in the pure white linen robe common to the priesthood (not in his own gorgeous robe of high-priestly office), and he always bore the blood of atonement in his hands. Thus has Christ ascended in purity and victory, and ever intercedes for us in the heavens. The *personal* glory of Christ is set forth in many sublime passages. (See Song of Sol. v. 10–16; Ezek. i. 26; Dan. vii. 9–13, x. 5, 6; Rev. i. 13–16, vi. 2, xix. 11–13.) The *official* glory of Christ is also set forth in wondrous splendor. (See Isa. vi. 3, marg.; cf. John xii. 41; Phil. iv. 19.) The personal and official *fullness* of Christ are linked together in most blessed and encouraging union. The fountain, river, and ocean can only faintly show what fullness of blessing He contains. (See John i. 14; Col. i. 19, ii. 9; Eph. iv. 13.)

XLIX

PLAINS OF MOAB—THE PRAYER OF MOSES

ANOTHER matter of very great interest and importance engages our attention at this last station of the journey. It is the prayer of Moses, so touching in itself, and so wide-reaching in its lessons and consequences. The account of it we have in Deuteronomy, the third chapter, from the twenty-third verse to the end. Moses declares, "I besought the Lord at that time, saying, O Lord God, Thou hast begun to show Thy servant Thy greatness, and Thy mighty hand: for what God is there in heaven or in earth, that can do according to Thy works, and according to Thy might? I pray Thee, let me go over, and see the good land that is beyond Jordan, that goodly mountain, and Lebanon. But the Lord was wroth with me for your sakes, and would not hear me: and the Lord said unto me, Let it suffice thee; speak no more unto Me of this matter."

If you will look at the last verse of the chapter you will see that Moses gives one reason for their long tarrying in the valley over against Beth-peor. It was to give space for the uttering of this prayer, and the answer which God was pleased to give. Evidently this was a very important prayer, as showing to Israel and to all the world what God's purposes are in such cases. Notice:

1. *It was a simple prayer.*

Moses comes to God as a child would go to a father. He speaks straight out of his heart. He bases his plea upon God's past goodness, and from this argues that that goodness will surely be shown to him in the future. Thus should we pray, coming to the Father in childlike spirit, basing our petitions upon His past benefits, which are thankfully acknowledged, and being confident that His promises are yea and amen in Christ, even to the end of time.

2. *It was a selfish prayer.*

In this was its shortcoming. In a sense Moses was right in asking that this thing might be done for him, and yet the prayer was very different from the former petitions we have heard falling from his lips. "Let *me* go over," he says; "let *me* see the good land." There is just a trace of selfish impatience in this, because Moses already knew that God had purposed to exclude him from actually treading Canaan. Let us avoid prayers in which the self is prominent. Childish selfishness and impatience enter not into acceptable childlikeness.

3. *Yet Moses ascribed glory to God.*

"What God is there in heaven or in earth, that can do according to Thy works, and according to Thy might?" These words were very fitting upon the lips of Moses. In his hours of silence and meditation he had had abundant opportunity to study God's ways and works. Constantly in the desert, as he led the people, he beheld the greatness of God in creation and providence. From this we should learn that one element of true childlikeness consists in observing what the Father has done and is doing, and that it is proper for us to render glory to Him for all that we observe. A loving child does this toward an earthly parent, and this is a part of the essence of prayer.

4. *It was a specific prayer.*

There was none of the indefiniteness about it which too often destroys the force of modern prayer. The specific desire was voiced to go over to see the good land; to look upon the goodly mountain especially, and to behold the glories of Lebanon particularly. All these things are mentioned with definiteness. What they imported will be more fully seen in our next study. Meanwhile let us learn the importance of definiteness in prayer. Peter did not put a preamble and preface to what he had to ask when he was sinking in the waters. " Lord, save me; I perish," he cried. Paul did not indulge in circumlocution when the Master revealed Himself on the way to Damascus. " Lord, what wilt Thou have me to do?" he asked. So with all the other Bible saints. Elias "prayed in his prayer" (James v. 17, marg.). Too many of us do not *pray* in our prayer. We say prayers, or we mumble in prayer, or we offer complimentary ascriptions in prayer, or we compass sea and land to make a beautiful prayer, whereas we should *pray* in our prayer. Notice the beautiful thing which the psalmist says of himself: " I am prayer " (Ps. cix. 4, omit italics). In another place he says, " I am peace " (Ps. cxx. 7). The one statement is the cause, the other is the result. If we are "all prayer," as the meaning is, we will be "all peace."

5. *The prayer of Moses was denied in part.*

"The Lord was wroth with me; He was wroth for your sakes." That is to say, through yielding to the petulant people, Moses had grown petulant himself. By not reprimanding them in their sin, he had sinned himself. Instead of speaking to the rock as commanded, he had struck it; instead of giving all glory to God, he had arrogated a part of the glory to himself. "Must *we* bring water out of the rock for you?" he demanded. Therefore God "would not hear"; that is to say, He did not answer as Moses desired. But the Father is always the best judge of what the child requires. The wise earthly father takes his boy out of the fields where he has been joyously pursuing the gay butterflies, and where he fain would always remain, and puts him in school and afterward sends him to college. The boy may think it hard at first, but at length he sees the wisdom of the plan, and years thereafter lays the laurel of his triumphs in tearful gratitude upon his father's grave. So God knew best. Moses needed to be humbled because of his sin, and so God said to him, "Thou shalt not go over this Jordan." Moses needed to learn also that the law is weak and cannot bring the soul through Jordan—that is to say, "the river of judgment" or "God's justice"—into the heavenly Canaan. This is the work of Joshua or Jesus, who is the real propitiation (1 John ii. 2).

6. *The prayer was granted in part.*

He was not allowed to *go over* to see, but he saw. Something better than he had asked was given him.

Without the fatigue and danger of the work of conquest, Moses was allowed in spirit to enter into the delights of the good land. Let us never forget that when God seems to deny our petitions, when fervently and faithfully uttered, it is in order that He may grant us something far better. No wise parent will give to his child "a razor without a handle," as Dr. Stephen Alexander used to say.

7. *The result in true submission of heart.*

God laid hard things upon Moses. "Get thee up to the top of Pisgah," He said. That was hard enough because of what was to be his fate upon Pisgah. But something harder follows: "Charge Joshua, encourage him and strengthen him, for he shall go over." It is always hard to resign a cherished wish in favor of another. It is difficult to say, "He must increase, but I must decrease." But this Moses was required to say. Nobly and splendidly did he encourage and strengthen Joshua and all the people, as we may read in the Book of Deuteronomy from the fourth chapter on to the end. What sublime submission to the will of God! What beautiful humility resulting from apparently unanswered prayer! May we learn to exercise the same toward God whether He hear us or seem to deny. And may we learn from this petition of Moses that the great desire of all souls should be to breathe the air of the heavenly Canaan, to go on unto perfection, to see and possess the goodly mountain of Lebanon, and thus through fellowship in Christ's suffering to be made partakers of His resurrection and glory. Oh, that we might hunger and thirst after righteousness! Then would we come unto Him to eat and drink (John vii. 37, 38).

L

PLAINS OF MOAB—THE VISION OF MOSES

It was no new thing for Moses to be called up to the mountain-top to meet with God. On the heights of Midian he had seen the burning bush. On the heights of Sinai he had been surrounded by the burning cloud. Here upon the top of Nebo Moses finds himself once more in an especial manner in the very presence of God, and before his eyes are unfolded such visions as even he had never beheld before. Very wonderful and very significant was the panorama of actual Canaan and of typical Canaan spread out before him. On the top of the "exceeding high mountain" our Lord was caused to see "all the kingdoms of the world, and the glory of them"; on one of the lonely hills outside of Jerusalem Isaiah was permitted to behold visions showing the downfall of Babylon, Moab, and Damascus; on the mountains of Patmos, John, the beloved disciple, beheld all the wonders of history and the marvelous unfolding of the divine purposes and judgments to the end of time. Along with these visions should be placed that which God caused Moses to see from the top of Nebo.

1. *He saw the good land.*

His power of vision was clarified and rendered telescopic, so that he could take in the whole of Canaan, the pleasant and fruitful country. And as he gazed God said sweetly in his ear, " This is the land which I sware unto Abraham, unto Isaac, and unto Jacob, saying, I will give it unto thy seed " (Deut. xxxiv. 4). It is expressly said that he showed him " all the land of Gilead," which stood on the east side of Canaan, even " unto Dan," a city on the northern border, " and all the land of Judah," which is in the southern part, even " unto the utmost sea," that is, the Mediterranean, which bounded Canaan on the west. All this God caused him to see, and therefore it is evident that it was a vision, and not a mere limited sweep of the natural sight. How much this must have meant to Moses! All through their wanderings they had been dreaming of Canaan, anticipating the milk from its herds and the honey flowing out of its rocks and tree-trunks. And now, although he might not step upon its soil, he beheld the " good land " and saw that God's promises are sure.

2. *He saw the exploits that were to result in the capture of the land.*

This we may fairly infer from the facts of the spiritual vision which evidently was given him. We are confirmed in this inference by the Targum of Jonathan and Solomon Ben Jarchi, who record the ancient Jewish belief that Moses had a vision of all that the judges, leaders, and kings were to do in the conquering of the nations and the settling of the several tribes, till the sanctuary at last had been built and destroyed. The prophetic gift unto this eminent servant of God was doubtless made clear at this moment, and he saw straight on through all that God should do through Joshua, the man, and Jesus, the Son of man.

3. *He saw Mount Zion.*

It is evident that the goodly mountain which he desired to behold was none other than Zion. One hundred and twenty-six times in the Bible is Zion referred to as the mountain which God loves, where God dwells, and out of which salvation flows. It was famous for its morning dews and its evening views. The Son of God is represented as standing upon Mount Zion when first God said to Him, "Thou art My Son; this day have I begotten Thee" (Ps. ii. 6, 7). Zion thus stands for the sacrifice of Christ, the Lamb slain from the foundation of the world; it stands for the second covenant, completed in His blood (Gal. iv. 24, 26); it stands for heaven itself, into which we enter through the blood (Heb. xii. 22). No wonder, therefore, that Moses desired to see Mount Zion. What sweet hopes must have entered into his heart as he looked upon those heights, afterward to be crowned with the temple and to be trodden by the feet of the incarnate Son of God!

4. *He saw Mount Lebanon.*

If Mount Zion was the image of the perfection of beauty in Christ as the sacrifice, Lebanon was the type of the sweet and refreshing benefits flowing from Him. The sweet odors from Lebanon and the streams of clear water issuing from the mountain-side are frequently used in the Bible to typify the blessings proceeding from Christ's life and work (Song of Sol. iv. 11). Indeed, the very name of Lebanon means "the heart of the Son" or "the heart of the Eternal One." "In Him are hid all the treasures of wisdom and knowledge"

(Col. ii. 3). We may well imagine that the odors from Lebanon cheered Moses' spiritual senses, and that by faith he drank of the living streams gushing from the mountain-side.

Let us do the same. When thinking of Christ let us often whisper gratefully, "All Thy garments smell of myrrh, and aloes, and cassia, out of the ivory palaces" (Ps. xlv. 8). Myrrh stands for sweetness, aloes for bitterness, and cassia for healing. Christ manifests sweetness, endured much bitterness, and brings spiritual healing to the world.

5. *He saw the failure of the law.*

He had fulfilled his mission as a man and as a type; he had led the people long and faithfully; he had stood for justice and judgment; but his star was now to set before the rising sun of Joshua. The law fails to lead to Canaan, and Moses must have been deeply impressed with the fact—more deeply than any one else has ever been.

6. *He saw judgment upon sin.*

From Nebo he went back in thought to Kadesh. How conscious he must have been of his own shortcoming at that moment of supreme privilege when he stood before the rock to call water forth for the people! What a grievous thing his own sin must have appeared to him here on Nebo! And from this how he must have gone on to a vivid appreciation of the guilt of sin in general! Such visions of sin and its consequences have come to holy men in the past and come to them still.

Enoch prophesied, saying, "Behold, the Lord cometh with ten thousand of His saints, to execute judgment upon all" (Jude 14, 15); and Daniel in his sleep beheld "till the thrones were cast down, and the Ancient of days did sit, and the Son of man came with the clouds of heaven" (Dan. vii. 9, 13). Such a vision as this God gave to Moses, vision of the great day which God hath appointed when He will judge the world by Jesus Christ. It is worthy of remark that the word "Gilead" mentioned in the passage before us means "eternity revealed," and that "Dan" means "the judgment." In this we may see a suggestion of the wideness of the vision Moses beheld, for he saw all the way from Gilead to Dan.

7. *He saw God's purposes of grace.*

The voice from heaven said to John, "Come up hither, and I will show thee things that must be hereafter." The voice of God, speaking to Moses, promised the same thing. Once before God had said to him, "I will be gracious to whom I will be gracious, and will show mercy on whom I will show mercy" (Exod. xxxiii. 19). The humbled prophet on Nebo knew better what these words implied than he had ever known before. In spite of his sin God was gracious to him, and in the misery of conscious failure and unworthiness God showed him abundant mercy. So will it be with us. But in order to see these things we must rise above the world; we must get with Christ upon the mountain-tops; Nebo's solid rocks must be under our feet, and the clear air of exalted communion with heaven must be fanning our cheeks.

LI

PLAINS OF MOAB—THE DEATH OF MOSES

SLOWLY the vision which had been afforded him faded away, and before the eyes of Moses appeared nothing but the wide-spread camp of the Israelites beneath him. Then, "according to the word of the Lord," or, as the beautiful Hebrew is, "by the kiss of the Lord," Moses dies. How attractive to the imagination is the scene thus afforded of the last moments of the great leader and commander! Poetry has dwelt upon it with tenderness, eloquence has described its salient features and its practical lessons, and more than one heart has turned to it in the extremities of darkness and death. Yet, after all, what a simple scene it is! The life of Moses requires many chapters for its delineation, but the death of Moses is adequately described in a single verse. Let us learn from this that the life of a servant of God is the important thing in the eyes of God, and that death is its simple and fitting close. There are three main lessons to be drawn from the simple account before us as to the death of Moses and death in general:

1. *The necessity of it.*

"And the Lord spake unto Moses that selfsame day,

saying, Get thee up into this mountain Abarim, unto Mount Nebo, which is in the land of Moab, and die in the mount, and be gathered unto thy people; as Aaron thy brother died in Mount Hor, and was gathered unto his people" (Deut. xxxii. 48-50). Thus it will be seen that the death of Moses resulted from a distinct command; but the command was based upon the inevitable and was uttered in infinite wisdom. "As Aaron;" this is the way of all the world, and now Moses' time, the proper time, has come. So is our death arranged by infinite wisdom. The moment of it cannot be postponed, neither can it be unduly hastened. Every man is immortal till his work is done. (See Num. xxxi. 2.)

2. *The loneliness of it.*

It must have come as a distinct shock to Moses, after his singing the wonderful song of triumph which we have recorded in the thirty-second chapter of Deuteronomy, that God should say to him, without hesitation or prelude, "Get thee up into the mountain, and die." How much he must have wanted to take some friend with him! — Joshua or Caleb, who had been with him during all the desert experiences, or even one of the young men who had grown up around him as they had journeyed onward. But this was not to be. No eye but that of God could look upon his last moments. And so it is with us. What a blessing that we can truly say, "Yea, though I walk through the valley of the shadow of death, I will fear no evil: for Thou art with me; Thy rod and Thy staff they comfort me"!

3. *The peacefulness of it.*

One cannot read the simple narrative in the concluding chapter of Deuteronomy without being touched with the thought that Moses died in absolute peace. His sins had been forgiven him, his work was done, the revelations of God's purposes were completed, and there was nothing more for him to do than to smile his childlike gratitude for the Father's good-night kiss, and then to fall asleep. This peacefulness grew out of three things.

(*a*) He had seen the "good land," and knew that, as Canaan meant rest from all the enemies of the desert, so he was about to enter into rest from all the enemies of his soul.

(*b*) He had beheld Joshua, who was to succeed him and was to typify before all the people the work of the great Saviour of mankind. Hence the peace of Moses had in it something of the faith and composure of Simeon when he said, "Lord, now lettest Thou Thy servant depart in peace: for mine eyes have seen Thy salvation" (Luke ii. 29, 30).

(*c*) The presence of the Lord was, after all, the real cause of his peaceful exit. In many trying times God had been with him in the past, and now Moses felt confident that all was well. Let us cultivate a keen observation of God's grace and goodness in all the affairs of life, that at death we may have perfect confidence in Him, and that thus our minds may have perfect peace because they are "stayed upon Him" (Isa. xxvi. 3).

"Them that sleep in Jesus," or, as the Greek has been rendered, "Them that are hushed to sleep in or by Jesus" (1 Thess. iv. 14); this is the appropriate epitaph of all God's saints. They "sleep," as Isaiah says, "resting in their beds" (Isa. lvii. 2). They repose in a chamber which Jesus has "locked with the key of peace, and will open with the key of the resurrection." We need not repine, though "it is appointed unto men once to die" (Heb. ix. 27). Death is the destroyer of happiness, but Jesus is the destroyer of death (Luke vii. 11–16). The sad record in all parts of the world is, "And he died." (See all through Gen. v., even in the case of Methuselah.) But what matters it? We have victory in our Lord. Let us not try to get comfort out of Asa's perfumed tomb (2 Chron. xvi. 14), or out of the carven mausoleums of the kings (Isa. xiv. 18), or out of Shebna's costly and resplendent sepulcher (Isa. xxii. 16). Let our cry ever be, "Thanks be to God, who giveth us the victory through our Lord Jesus Christ" (1 Cor. xv. 57).

LII

PLAINS OF MOAB—THE MOURNING FOR MOSES

ACCORDING to the Jewish tradition, the death of Moses occurred in the seventh month, Adar, which is toward the end of our February. Out of an impulse of affection rather than by any direct command of God, they tarried still in the plains of Moab for thirty days, mourning the loss of their great leader (Deut. xxxiv. 8). This, indeed, seems already to have become a custom with them; for we read that they mourned during a similar period for Aaron when he died (Num. xx. 29). God allowed them to tarry during these thirty days, seeing, doubtless, that it was wise that they should do so. The infinite Father does not interfere with the natural impulses of affection until that course is necessary in order to prevent harm resulting. In the first chapter of the Book of Joshua we read that when it became possible that the Israelites should become slothful and inactive through their mourning, God said sharply to them, "Moses My servant is dead; now therefore arise, go over this Jordan." But during these thirty days God allowed them to weep in peace, in order that the lessons of the death of His great servant might sink into their hearts; yet He took care that no false opinions should spread among the people.

1. *He hid away the body of Moses in order to prevent superstition.*

"No man knoweth of his sepulcher unto this day." There is something mysterious and awe-inspiring in the announcement; but we can see the wisdom of this procedure. The poor lifeless body of even so good and great a man as Moses is not of importance. Yet, had it remained in the possession of the people, they would doubtless have made it an object of superstition and idolatry. They had done this with the brazen serpent already, perhaps. The people certainly elevated the mere symbol into something of superstitious importance afterward. (See 2 Kings xviii. 4.)

2. *God taught them that they must leave the ministration of the law.*

They were now to follow Joshua, and in a measure they were to forget the things that were behind and to press on with new courage and purpose into the opening period which was to prefigure the coming of Christ. This lesson we must return to again and again, for it is the one important matter to be noted in these closing moments of the desert experience.

3. *Yet observe that the law is not entirely abrogated when Moses died.*

He, standing as the personification of the law, was a hundred and twenty years old, yet "his eye was not dim, nor his natural force abated," by which is signified that the law still abides in force and living vigor. All are under condemnation while they live in sin, for "the law hath dominion over a man as long as he liveth," but when we are dead to sin then the law becomes dead to us. "We become dead to the law by the body of Christ; that we should be married to another, even to Him who is raised from the dead" (Rom. vii. 1–4). The people were still upon the desert side of Jordan, hence they were still under the law.

4. *We learn that we may pass beyond the desert dispensation.*

The people were to pass through Jordan and come into new and more pleasant experiences. This we may do as well. If we forget the things that are behind, we should press on to follow our Jesus through the Jordan, or the baptism of suffering, until He gives us our true rest (Phil. iii. 13). "Take My yoke upon you, and learn of Me; for I am meek and lowly in heart: and ye shall find rest unto your souls" (Matt. xi. 29). He *gives* us the rest of justification when we believe on Him; but we *find* the rest of sanctification when we take the yoke and follow Him through the Jordan into perfect consecration.

5. *To come to this rest we must die unto the law.*

This has already been hinted at. It is typified in the passing through Jordan. The Jews regarded that as the type of death, and the coming up on the other side as the symbol of the resurrection. Thus are we baptized into the death of Christ in order that we may know the power of His resurrection. On the Canaan side we are no longer under the law, but under grace. "The law of the Spirit of life hath made us free from the law of sin and death" (Rom. viii. 2).

6. *All this cannot come about without sore struggle.*

The people weeping for thirty days before Mount Nebo show us in vivid type the strong crying and tears which precede the death of the self-life. Oh, what sad struggles with self and sin in the poor human heart! What bitter debates as to those things which need to be "given up"! What sorrowful anticipations of possible failure and dismay precede the plunge into Jordan! You will remember that the people of Israel were still encamped so that one wing of their host was guarded by Abel-shittim and the other by Beth-jesimoth, the one meaning "the sorrow of scourges" and the other "the house of desolation." This is the best that the law can do for us. It brings us into the place of sorrow and struggle, of penitence and tears.

7. *But the result is righteousness and peace.*

Jesus, our new leader, shows Himself unto us as the Lord's salvation indeed; coming to save us from our enemies and from the hands of all that hate us, that we may "serve Him without fear, in holiness and righteousness, all the days of our life" (Luke i. 74, 75).

No soul has ever come to the valley of decision fronting Jordan without experiencing something of the temptations and struggles hinted at in these concluding lessons. Bitterly does Satan dispute every inch of the ground we make toward the baptism of full consecration. Fightings within, allurements without, Moabites to smile upon us, Midianites to attack us, losses to appal, and bitter tears to be shed—all these things befall him who would follow Jesus without reserve. It is a heavy price to pay, but what we gain is worth all the cost. Oh yes, the half cannot be told of the sweet peace and the satisfying righteousness we come into, as a priceless heritage, in the Canaan of full surrender!

Come, soul, let us step together into Jordan. "We would see Jesus;" we would enter into the territory of the King. Let us not shiver and shrink any longer on the brink of the river. With our first step the waters shall divide, and, behold, we come into "quietness and assurance forever"!

Or, if Jordan mean death to you, the same promise may be made. We have walked together all the long way from Rameses, "the washing away of evil," to the stream that separates from the "land of far distances." Step forward, soul, and fear not! Thy Joshua leads thee. He has pledged Himself to meet thee midway. The waters shall not overflow thee. Before thou knowest thou shalt be in the Canaan all-glorious, met and welcomed by the radiant host of loved ones gone before! "Let us be glad and rejoice, and give honor to Him" (Rev. xix. 7).